Textiles Transformed

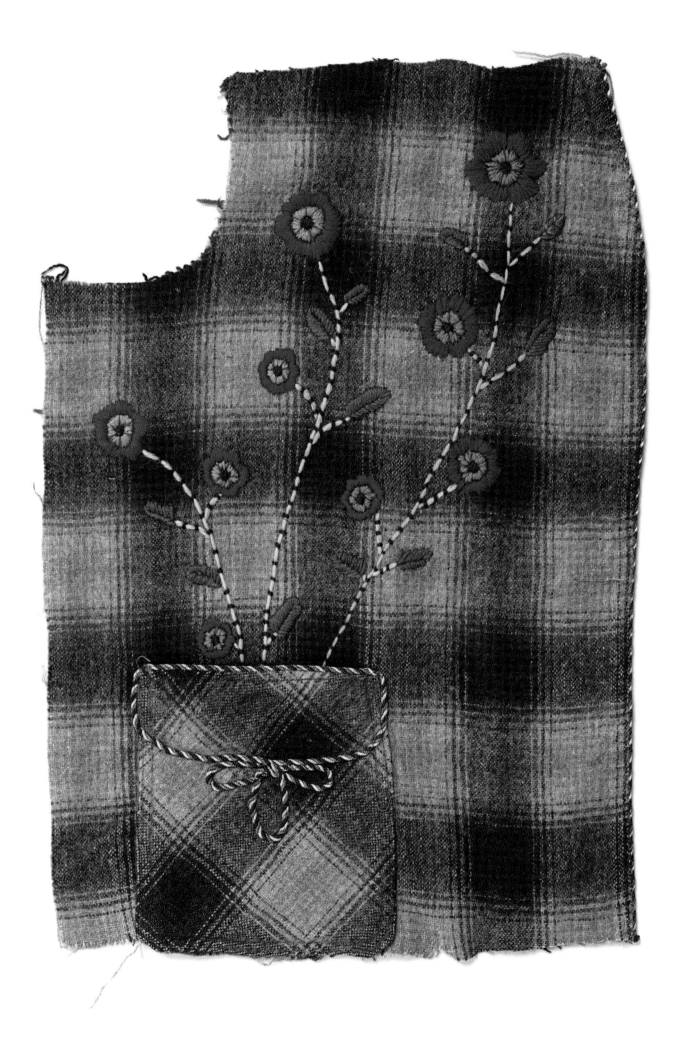

Textiles Transformed

Thread and Thrift with
Reclaimed Textiles

Mandy Pattullo

BATSFORD

First published in the United Kingdom in 2020 by
Batsford
43 Great Ormond Street
London WC1N 3HZ
An imprint of Pavilion Books Company Ltd

Copyright © B T Batsford Ltd, 2020
Text © Mandy Pattullo, 2020

ISBN: 9781849945806

A CIP catalogue record for this book is available from the British Library.

25 24 23 22 21
10 9 8 7 6 5 4 3

Reproduction by Rival Colour, UK
Printed by Toppan Leefung, China

This book can be ordered direct from the publisher at the website:
www.pavilionbooks.com, or try your local bookshop.

Contents

Introduction

I rent a studio in a converted manse (clergyman's house) in a pretty village in Northumberland in the north of England. Having worked hard all my life as a teacher, surface pattern designer and mother, I feel I have earned this room of my own where I can surround myself with beautiful fabrics and threads, plug in my headphones and lose myself in constructing textile collages and hand stitching. I seem to have been collaging my whole life, whether that be in the scrapbooks I have been making since I was a young child, creating mood boards for clients and students, curating the mantlepiece in my home or sorting my fabrics into bundles of interesting combinations.

I work by hand because I choose to, and I have a deep need to employ my hands to some practical purpose. I garden, cook, sew and play the piano, but making a stitch and patching together pieces of cloth is absolutely integral to who I am. I was probably sewing when I met my husband more than forty years ago and my children would think it odd not to see me combining stitching with having a conversation, watching the TV or relaxing on holiday. I love the whole process: gathering and searching out lovely things, creating colour stories and moods, deciding on the composition and surface decoration and then creating something new. It is not just the slowness of stitching by hand and being 'in the zone' when doing it that I love, but also about the power of transforming something by making my own mark on it.

I use a carefully selected collection of old and worn textiles that have been gifted to me or have been sourced at antique textile fairs and flea markets. These are beautiful textiles that hold within them their own story and you might ask why I feel the need to decorate them, cut them up and reassemble them into new pieces. I often wonder why myself, but I think it is about changing the textile surface, taking ownership of it and then re-presenting it so it transforms from something someone once made or wore into a new piece of my own. If I just kept the textiles folded and stored I would probably not look at them very often, but by interacting with them over a period of time I build up a relationship with the cloth and the previous maker as I unpick their stitches, deconstruct their garment or embroidery and use it for myself. The resolved textile piece is then shared and talked about with those who come into my studio, shared to a wider audience across the world through social media and then might act as an inspirational sample to those I teach. Is this not a better thing than the original being seen and owned by only me?

I hesitate to use the words upcycling or recycling in relation to what I do as I do not really make anything that is useful or serves a purpose. I prefer to apply the word *reworking* as I am using what I have found, items that have had a previous life and, in the end, what I make doesn't have to be useful if it feeds my soul and is a sustainable craft technique. In this book I hope to convey some of the excitement I feel at the transformative process of changing a textile piece, and encourage you to do the same. You will not be able to re-create what I do as everything I source and make is unique, but I hope I can give you the confidence to have a go and inspire you to rework things you own, to find in them the tender details and add a few of your own.

Above and right:
Work in progress
at my studio in
Northumberland.

The Basics

Fabrics

You will see that I mostly work with beautiful old fabrics and pieces of quilt. Some of the fabrics are inherited or gifted, many are charity-shop garments or family clothing, such as my husband's worn-out shirts, that have been taken apart. I try to work using only what I already have. Look in charity shops for blankets, domestic embroidered items, headscarves and quality vintage garments. For truly vintage and antique textiles, including quilts, I make special trips to vintage textile fairs, auctions, flea markets and brocantes. I do not expect to get something for nothing and am always willing to pay a reasonable amount for a quilt or exquisite piece of embroidery that I know both my students and I can make the most of. There are lots of people selling vintage textiles through Ebay, Etsy and Instagram now, so if you are committed to having a go at making work like that illustrated in this book, search it out and start to assemble a collection. You can also 'age' new fabric if you knock back the colour by dipping it in a tea solution or overdyeing using natural dyes that are not damaging to the environment. You might like to mix in some more contemporary fabrics such as patchwork cottons; companies like French General (see page 125) have quilting fabrics inspired by beautiful antique French designs that I find mix well with my genuinely antique pieces.

Below and right: The sort of fabrics I collect include recycled clothing scraps, wool and quilt pieces.

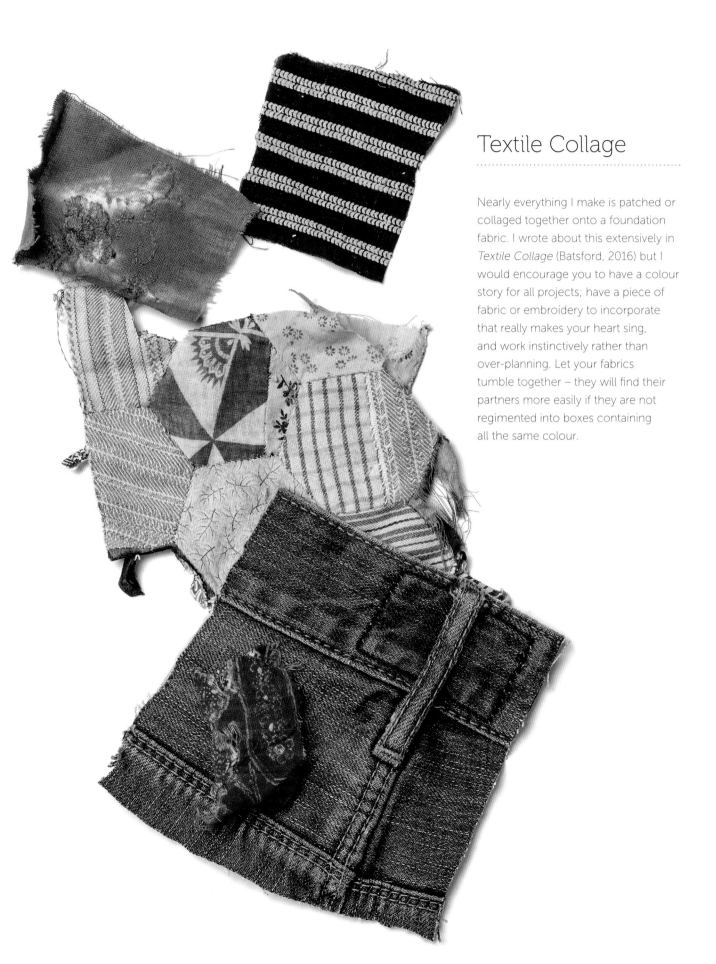

Textile Collage

Nearly everything I make is patched or collaged together onto a foundation fabric. I wrote about this extensively in *Textile Collage* (Batsford, 2016) but I would encourage you to have a colour story for all projects; have a piece of fabric or embroidery to incorporate that really makes your heart sing, and work instinctively rather than over-planning. Let your fabrics tumble together – they will find their partners more easily if they are not regimented into boxes containing all the same colour.

Foundations and Attaching

I do not like to embroider within a hoop so everything I work with has to have a foundation fabric firm enough that the stitching will not pull the fabric collage out of shape. I increasingly use a bonded curtain lining, which is fabric on one side with a wadding bonded on to it, and I place the collage materials on the fuzzy wadding side. I find as I stitch together and embroider on to this sort of backing it quilts it as the stitches sink into the two layers underneath. I also use wool felt, old blanket and pieces of thin quilt as foundations for patchworking on to. If you are working with a garment you do not need to consider a background, though if the fabric of the garment is thin or woollen you might need to stretch it into a frame while you work on it.

Everything I make is hand stitched and, unless I have chosen to turn the edges, everything is sewn on to the foundation or garment with either a stab stitch just within the edge of the cloth, or an overcast stitch over the edge of the cloth. You could also attach with buttonhole stitch, cross stitch or herringbone stitch. In the diagrams, the attaching stitches are very obvious, but in reality I use the same colour thread as the fabric to make the stitches as invisible as possible. If I have chosen to turn the edge of the fabric I am appliquéing I use slipstitch in the traditional way.

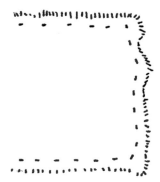

Stab stitch just inside the border.

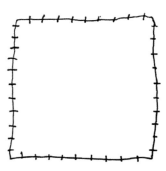

Overcast stitch over the border.

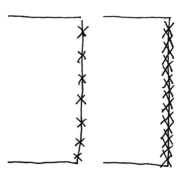

Cross stitch and herringbone stitch.

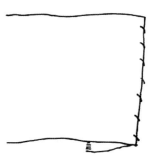

Slipstitch for finger-turned appliqué.

Needles and Pins

I use good-quality sewing needles and change them frequently, particularly if I am sewing into a piece of old quilt, as I find they are blunted by the wadding. I also use fine pins and like to use those without coloured heads as I find the colour distracting when I am composing a piece.

Threads

My threads, unlike my fabrics, are arranged by colour and I use all types of threads apart from very slippery and shiny rayons. I mostly use stranded embroidery thread (floss), coton à broder and coton perle no. 8. I supplement these with some old silk threads I have sourced from French markets and the internet. When I am working on to wool I nearly always use wool threads, particularly crewel and tapestry wools. For fine stitching I might use ordinary sewing thread, the type you would use on a sewing machine.

Stitch

I love hand stitching but use a limited repertoire of stitches. I find that the stitches listed below give me all the marks I need to make. There are plenty of embroidery instruction books on the market and tutorials online, but before you start a project, if you do not know the stitches, practise first before stitching into your cloth.

I use the stitches to decorate the surface, to blend boundaries by working the stitches across patchworks and I also often heavily repeat stitches, scattering them liberally across a surface. The ones I most frequently use fall into different groups.

Straight stitches: running stitch, backstitch, stem stitch, satin stitch, fern stitch, seed stitch, long stitch, short stitch.

Crossed stitches: cross stitch, St George's cross stitch, herringbone stitch.

Chained stitches: chain stitch, lazy-daisy stitch, wheatear stitch.

Looped stitches: feather stitch, buttonhole stitch, fly stitch.

Knotted stitches: French knots, bullion knots.

Couching: In couching, a long stitch is laid across the fabric and small stitches are worked over the top of the thread to fasten it in place. Traditionally, the long stitch is made with a thick or precious thread (metallic) and the small stitches worked with a thinner or standard thread but you can use the same thread for both.

Opposite: The embroidered flowers have been attached with overcast stitch.

Left: The stems on these appliquéd flowers have been couched on using a contrasting colour of thread.

CHAPTER ONE

Quilt Love

Antique and vintage patchwork quilts can be lovely displayed on a bed but many that I source to use are very worn, dirty, unfinished or not to my taste. I transform them by cutting them up and using pieces within my collage work, stitching into them, using them as a base for appliqué and deconstructing them to create new fabrics. Using old quilts has been at the heart of my practice for a very long time and I am as in love with quilts now as I was in 1977 when I first started to make my own. Over the years I have shared many pieces of patchwork and quilting with students, and I like to think I have encouraged them to appreciate the workmanship of the original quilt but then to change its use and place their own marks on to the surface. This chapter encourages you to do the same.

Left: Detail from a
scroll-style fabric book
(see pages 26–27)

About Quilts

There is some confusion as to the difference between a quilt and a coverlet so I think it is worth defining this more clearly. A quilt is a sandwich of three layers: fabric, wadding, fabric. The top and bottom cloth and wadding are held together with either stitches or tying. A quilt can be:

Wholecloth: the top fabric is one big piece of cloth.

Strippy: patchwork strips run down the length of the quilt. This type of quilt was common in the North East of England where I work.

Patchwork: little pieces of fabric sewn together to form a whole. Patchwork can be made using a single shape such as a hexagon or diamond repeated, or can be made in blocks, or assembled in a 'crazy' fashion. A frame quilt has a central design surrounded by a border, but is still patchwork.

A coverlet, on the other hand, is made of two layers with no wadding. It can still be patchwork and the front and back can still be sewn together with familiar quilting patterns. Coverlets are thinner so are much easier to embroider on to.

It is not easy to source antique quilts, but there are many people now selling small pieces online and these are suitable for experimenting with and having a go at projects similar to those I am going to describe. I use my quilts in a number of ways, depending on the overall colour, what sort of state they are in and how thick the wadding is.

- A piece of quilt can act as a foundation on which to build up a textile collage or appliqué.

- The quilt can be deconstructed through unpicking or cutting away printed fabrics for other uses. This is particularly helpful if you are using a quilt with a very thick wadding as that can be discarded and the patchwork top retained.

- A piece of quilt, and especially coverlets, are a great surface on which to embroider.

- Turn the quilt over. The back might be more interesting than the front.

- Quilts can be upcycled into other products such as bags, brooches, fabric books or cushions.

Above: From left; tailors' samples quilt, Durham wholecloth quilt, log-cabin quilt, strippy quilt and patchwork coverlet.

Quilts as a Base
for Textile Collage

I demonstrated approaches to textile collage in my first book (*Textile Collage*, Batsford, 2016). It is perhaps enough just to remind you that collage is a word we associate with paper, meaning an assemblage of different elements usually glued to a background. Textile collage is about using a variety of fabrics and textures and applying them to a fabric background. In collaging with paper, text might play an important part and with textiles this could be translated into using perhaps pieces with print or embroidery on them to give surface interest against plainer fabrics. Like paper collage, edges can be torn or cut. In traditional collage the artist may add a further layer of marks through drawing or painting, and with my version, the marks are made with stitches.

A piece of quilt is an ideal foundation on which to build layers of fabric, and your main decision will be whether you are going to cover the surface completely or whether you will allow some of that precious base layer to show. In my log-cabin series of collages I have allowed the red central square to peek out, though on the whole I have obscured most of the beautiful silk patchwork. The red at the centre of the log-cabin block was traditionally supposed to symbolize the heart of the home, and as home is also where my heart is I have worked around it. The collage ingredients are some of my favourite small scraps and I like the cross-cultural feel where Chinese, Indian, French and British vintage samples mix with pieces salvaged from garments, worn quilts, found embroidery and needlepoint pieces. These do not come together quickly but little piles of fabrics sit on the top of each block for several days before being cut up and laid out in many different combinations (recorded on my phone camera) before finally being pinned and attached. Often a coloured strip within the log-cabin block has set me off on a colour scheme, helping me to refine the story and lose some ingredients that do not fit into the scheme. All the pieces are attached with a discreet overcast stitch over the raw edges.

Left: Collages layered on to 16cm (6¼in) square log-cabin blocks from the Victorian era.

You do not have to use a piece of quilt as a base but could create a collage by using just a section of a quilt and combining it with other fabrics that you have. In my collage *Peacock* I have recycled several favourite pieces of fabric, attaching them to a base of felt and using as the focal point a bird image which has been unpicked from a very dilapidated turkey red quilt. I have taken this collage even further by adding some hexagon patchwork, and embroidered across the whole surface. The embroidery design was drawn on freehand with a water-soluble pen and then worked in backstitch. I often look at old embroidery transfers for ideas for surface stitching, using the linear elements of the design. I do not iron on the transfer as I have found it is sometimes difficult to get rid of the blue ink on the transfer patterns. I enlarge designs and freehand draw the stems on the collage until I am happy and add the petals and leaves as I go along. Erase water-soluble pen marks using the manufacturer's instructions.

Above: *Peacock*, 2018, 32 x 41cm (12¾ x 16¼in). A peacock unpicked from a turkey red quilt is the focal point of this collage with embroidery embellishment.

Right: *The Red House*, 2018, 67 x 35cm (26 x 14in). Cross stitch and appliqué on to the back of a piece of crazy quilt.

Turning Over

Sometimes the patchwork quilt surface may be too bright or patterned and fight against the ideas you have for it. This is particularly the case with crazy quilts. These quilts were made in Victorian times out of scraps of velvet, silk and damask and were intended to be eye-catching and opulent. They were often embroidered with motifs like flowers or animals, and the border of each patch might be emphasized with a herringbone or feather stitch. I do not like many of the crazy quilts I have seen but I do love the back of the one I have used here in *The Red House*. The quilt was constructed on to a base fabric and turning over revealed a patchwork of patterned fabrics with traces and shadows of the stitches that embellished it. This has become the background for my piece.

My mother did cross stitch all her life and I have inherited her threads, books and patterns. I always rather despised it, thinking it was prescriptive and uncreative but my research into samplers and traditional folk patterns has made me change my mind. I like the way young girls practised their cross stitch, building up pictures of things that were important to them like houses, family and livestock. With the sale of the home I grew up in came a need to express this loss and using a beloved piece of quilt, my mother's

patterns, and marrying the two with my own textile collage technique, I have created a very personal piece of work. I did plan a little by overlaying a paper cross-stitch template of a house shape on to the quilt but after that I merely sewed a line of crosses, following a pattern a little, and then made it up as I got going. I have worked without a grid or a woven network to keep me straight and have not worried too much about the size or direction of the crosses. The addition of appliquéd flowers around the house has also helped to transform the reverse side of this rather ugly crazy quilt and combined the two traditions of my own textile collage visual language and that of my mother's cross stitching.

Always turn over a quilt and consider whether the back appeals to you more than the front. You don't need to do labour-intensive cross stitch like me but you can use it as a canvas for your own ideas.

The handwritten sketchbook notes read (best reading):

Wren

rusty brown colour with long pale stripe over the eye, pale breast and underside. Light brown bars on wings

Known as the king of birds won the title by flying higher than the eagle. Hid under the feathers of the eagle when it soared above the other birds. Tiny dumpy it pops out & flew just above him. Long thin bill and large feet

Energetic darts quickly from place to place

5-8 Eggs

Jenny Wren

Very loud distinctive song

small tail, dark mottled dark back

Troglodytes troglodytes   9-10.5cm

Garden Birds

I find that a piece of quilt is a very effective foundation on which to work in a more figurative way, and I particularly love to create portraits of the common birds that visit our gardens. I have many illustrated books about birds which I refer to, and I keep scrapbooks of illustrations taken from magazines and second-hand books. I also sometimes work in a sketchbook as this allows me to look at a number of pictures but then come up with something more original of my own. I am always aiming to capture the spirit and character of the bird rather than an exact imitation of an illustration, but it is important to keep the colours quite realistic so that the type of bird can be recognized.

Above: Sketchbook study of wrens, 2019. Mixed media.

How to make a bird portrait

1 Draw or photograph the bird you would like to portray and, when you are happy with the image or illustration, use a photocopier to alter the size if necessary. Stick the image to card and then create a template by drawing round it. You just need a silhouette to get you going.

2 Draw round the silhouette template on to a piece of quilt or other surface with a water-soluble pen. Think carefully about the placement of the template. Do you need to allow space for a branch? Is the bird standing on the ground?

3 Collect together small scraps of fabric, bearing in mind that you want to match the colours of the bird's plumage as accurately as you can. You can use any thin fabrics – patchwork cottons, old polyester scarves from charity shops, sheers and vintage – but nothing too thick.

4 Start to cut tiny fabrics to fit within the silhouette, always referring to a bird book for colour reference. This is not as easy as it seems as there is a lot of variation in the way artists paint birds and then there are differences between the male and female of the species, juveniles and older birds as well as seasonal changes. Some of my books are old and the pictures faded so I read the description of the plumage too instead of relying solely on the

picture. You will need to have clean-cut lines from the top of the head down the back of the bird to echo the sleekness but within the shape you should attempt a more feathery look to your cutting, making use of fraying edges. You will have lots of tiny pieces so you may want to lay them on with tweezers. Try to avoid straight edges within the shape and this is where sheers can be overlaid. You might want to leave some areas open or to stitch the colour in. For example, the pale streak over the eye of the wren is too fiddly to cut in fabric so I sometimes do this in stitch. Pin everything in place and then stitch down with tiny stab stitches. They will stay in the piece so they are not tacking stitches and need to be worked with a thread colour that matches the fabrics.

Below: Tiny pieces of fabric being pinned on to an old piece of quilt, with the water-soluble pen markings as a guide. A simple template has been used.

5 Now you are ready to embroider and this is where you can really try to capture the markings of the plumage and use your stitches to blend the fabric pieces effectively. I mostly use long-and-short stitch for this job but sometimes French knots for spots, arrow stitch or detached chain for tiny feathers and couching if I want a long sweeping line. I use smaller stitches for the fluffier parts of the bird and change colours if need be. I work in cotton à broder, perle and stranded embroidery threads. The eye is worked in satin stitch with a French knot in the middle and backstitch round the eye ring to define it a little more. I do the legs last and go back to a bird book for colour reference and to see how long they are in proportion to the rest of the bird.

6 I finish off by contextualizing the bird in some way. Sometimes I scatter tiny flowers around it, stitch a horizon line or a branch. I am led by the quilt and the negative space around the bird. Get rid of the water-soluble pen marking with a paint brush and water (or following the manufacturer's instructions), making sure you do it all round the edges even if you can't see it as it will creep out when dry. When totally dry, iron the surface. Make sure there are no water-soluble pen marks left as ironing over them can make them permanent.

Right (detail) and left: *Wren*, 2019, 26 x 15cm (10¼ x 6in). Textile collage on to a piece of antique quilt.

The eye Work vertical satin stitch until the desired size is achieved. Surround with an eye circle of backstitches and put a glint in the eye with a French knot.

The beak Keep shape authentic and work in three long stitches or use couching to create a curved beak.

The legs Start at the body and work down to the toes using backstitch. Remember, there are three toes at the front and one at the back. I usually put a tiny stitch at the end of each toe as a toenail.

Deconstruction

Very worn and disintegrating quilts and patchwork tops that have never been made into a quilt can't really be used on beds, or, because of their fragile state, turned into cushions or bags. The layers of the quilt, however, can be peeled back and used in other projects. There is something very satisfying about slowly unpicking a quilt or deconstructing the blocks of patchwork into separate elements. Unpicking reveals the tracery of stitches from past makers and you end up with a pile of fragile textures and fragments. The deconstructed quilt pieces can be used in collages, book forms, appliquéd on to garments or gathered and applied to another surface and re-quilted. Liz Jones likes to tear her pieces of unpicked quilt to create soft, fraying edges. She layers these up into petals for flowers in her ragged still-life compositions.

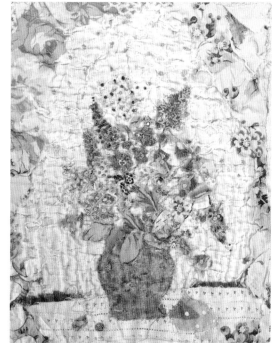

Above: Liz Jones,. *Torn*, 2019, 21 x 27cm (8¼ x 10½in). Scraps from a multi-layered antique quilt are attached with torn edges exposed in this still-life composition.

Left: *Red Coat*, 2018. A child's red wool coat has been embellished with a change of buttons and appliquéd flowers unpicked from a turkey red quilt.

Hannah Lamb

Hannah Lamb focuses on recording a sense of place through careful observation and material investigation. She works with a variety of processes including stitch, print, cyanotype and construction. She has a particular interest in archives and historical textiles.

[De]Constructed Cloth was created for and inspired by Sunny Bank Mills, a former textile mill near to Hannah's home in West Yorkshire. A visit to the archives and semi-derelict buildings on site coupled with recent visits to thriving local textile firms influenced ideas around the rise and fall of the industry. Ghostly cyanotype prints were first created on the length of cloth using deconstructed quilt pieces as stencils. Further layers of printing, dyeing, patching and deconstruction were used to develop complex layers of positive and negative imagery.

Below. Hannah Lamb, *[De]Constructed Cloth*, 2019, approx. 380 x 200 x 45cm (150 x 78 x 18in). Cyanotype, print and hand stitching on mixed-fibre fabric, with mirror and wooden bobbin.

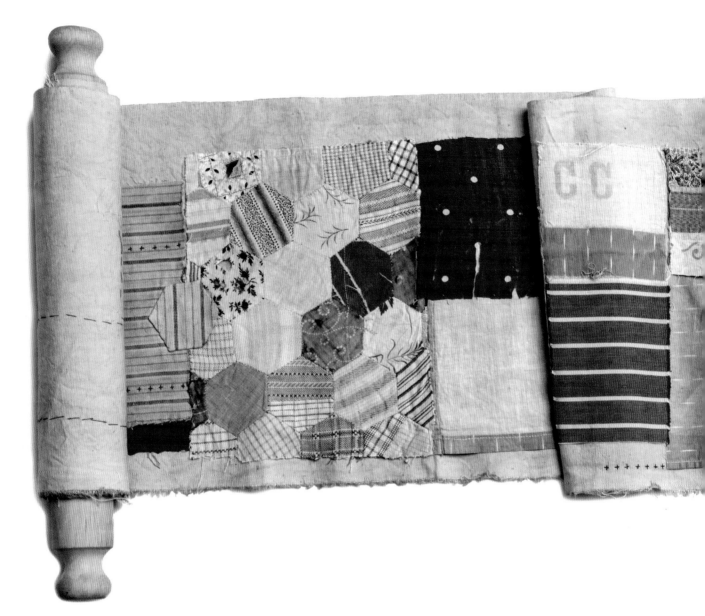

Book Forms

I like to use the fragile scraps from old quilts and patchwork tops to create book forms. In the scroll form, wrapped round a rolling pin, all of the elements are 'unpickings' from different quilts, but they have been brought together in a resolved linear narrative through a strict use of a colour story. They have been stab stitched on to a piece of French linen which I dyed to match the colour scheme. There are several pieces taken from turkey red quilts, which are perhaps my favourite sort of antique quilt as there were

so many beautiful block patterns used and the motifs are usually exquisitely drawn. If you are making your own scroll book, just bear in mind that it will not all be seen if it is partly unwrapped so that it is important the composition on the opening end is the best, as that is the bit that will be most frequently displayed. You could, of course, hang it up as a long wall hanging but you need to plan your pieces with this in mind as it will be viewed in a different way.

Rolling Pin Book, 2016, 265 x 28cm (104 x 11in). Unpicked and reclaimed vintage quilt fragments appliquéd and hand stitched on to dyed French linen and wrapped around a family rolling pin.

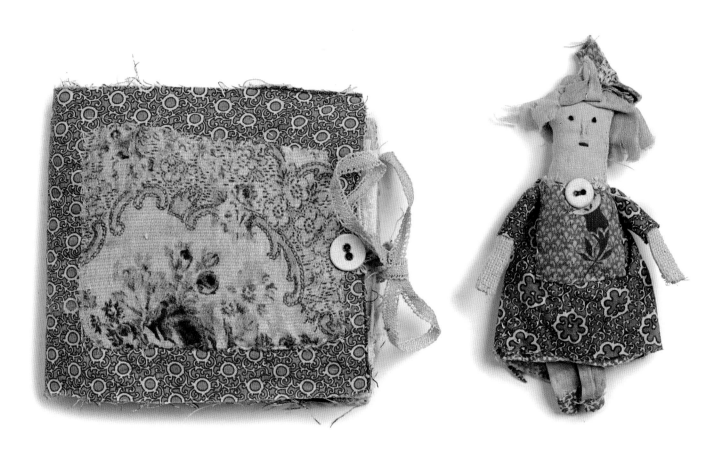

Above and right:
Rag Book, 2019,
8.5 x 9cm
(3¼ x 3½in).
The open book
reveals a concertina
structure that has
been attached at
the back into a
folded piece
of quilt.

Above right: *Rag
Doll*, 2019, 10cm
(4in) high. Every
component of
the doll, as with
the cover and the
contents of the
book, was made
by deconstructing
an old quilt and
revealing its
many layers.

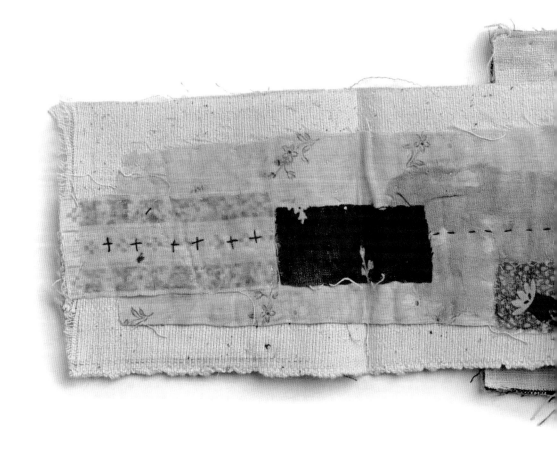

In the little concertina book all the fabrics were taken from deconstructing an A3 piece of quilt that was multi layered, having been recovered and remade by successive generations. The cover of the book was made from another piece of the original quilt top and the last page of the concertina was sewn on to the inside back of the folded quilt. This one has lace ties to hold it all together. There are some stitch details but really the story is about the ragged beauty and intimacy of the old fabric. I also made a tiny rag doll with the scraps that were left. The limbs on this little doll are so small that it would have been impossible to stitch up the inside seams and then turn them right side out, so instead I have rolled the fabric a little and whip stitched the two rolled edges together to get really little arms and legs. They are not stuffed but the body is stuffed with the tiny snippets of fabric offcuts from my desk. The body with the face is all one piece and was similarly whip stitched and then the limbs sewn on with a few stitches. The clothing was wrapped and sewn on to the body rather than it being clothing with which the doll could be dressed, and the hair has been made with tiny strips of quilt rags. The face is always the hardest thing to do but keep it simple as I have done here. I imagine in the past many children or mothers made dolls with the remnants of quilt-making fabrics.

Patchwork

I have come across many unfinished block and hexagon quilts where all that you have is the quilt top. It is not uncommon to find a partly finished quilt in a charity shop with a bag attached full of paper and fabric shapes. Most antique patchworks use many pieces of printed pattern and are a history, in themselves, of printed textile design as you see trends in textile design illustrated through the use of ditsy florals, geometrics, Indian paisleys and natural-form-inspired prints. I like to take the quilts apart and showcase my very favourite sections, and find the easiest way to do this is through mounting the pieces on to pages (sometimes another plain quilt piece). The pages are held together with buttons down the spine of the book. Visitors to my studios are able to look at the blocks easily by turning the pages, whereas it is unlikely they would take much in if I were to unfold the whole quilt top.

Above: *A Book of Stars*, 2018. Each page and cover are 30 x 22cm (12 x 8½in). 12 pages. The cover and pages are pulled together by the buttons down the spine. This means pages can easily be detached if an element is needed for another project.

Below: The pages are made from the back lining of a quilt where the turkey red quilt top has been detached badly, leaving the shadows of stitching. The stars have been appliquéd on with stab stitch.

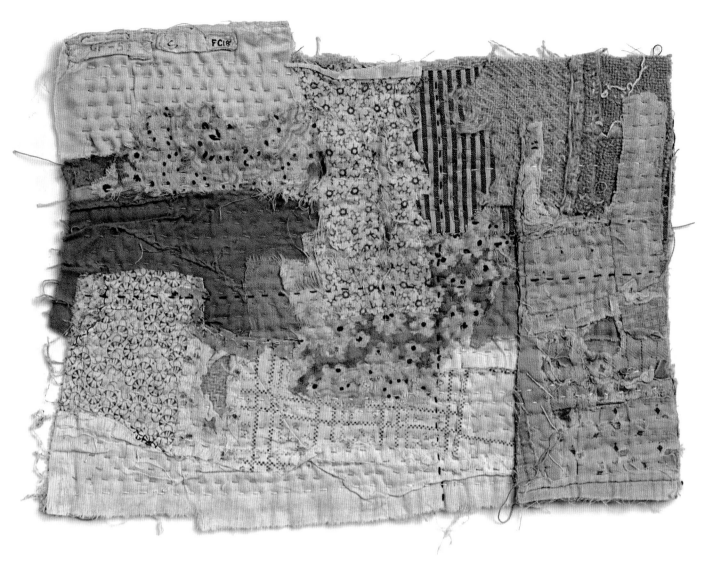

Take from a Tradition

Above: *Inspired by Kantha*, 2019. 29 x 21cm (11½ x 8¼in). Raggy pieces unpicked from quilts have been layered up and quilted together using two colours of running stitch.

I have an extensive collection of ethnic and historical textiles, which are used and on display in my own home. I particularly love old kanthas from the Eastern parts of India. They are a fantastic example of recycling as they are constructed through layering old saris and discarded cloth and sewing them together with many lines of running stitch to form a soft quilt or throw. They are easy to come by as there is an extensive industry in the making of them for tourists. If you are going to buy one then look for one that really does have layers of old fabrics and which shows signs of wear and tear. There are stories to be revealed in the fabrics and I like the way something beautiful is made out of something discarded. You can take this idea and do the same with the tiny fragile pieces you might have collected from deconstructing a very old quilt, though you could use other lightweight fabrics and muslins. Layer them on to a soft foundation and then just start enjoying the meditative process of building up the surface with repetitive stitching in order to attach them. In my example I have used running stitch in the spirit of the kantha makers and have also used a limited number of colours.

Quilt Words

A piece of quilt or coverlet can be an ideal basis on which to sew text and add meaning. This might be a favourite quote or line from a poem or something more personal, as I have shown in my own examples. The actual lettering can be formed using backstitch, stem stitch, cross stitch or couching. First I write the words or sentence out on tracing paper and overlay this on the background, moving words around until I am happy. I then transfer the text on to the quilt top using either a water-soluble pen or Frixion pen in my own handwriting or the method described opposite using carbon paper. If you are using the soluble-pen method then you might also want to draw a line with a ruler to get your lettering straight.

It sounds obvious, but I only use words when I actually have something to say and they have to have meaning. If you want to have a go at adding text to a collage, think carefully about the words and how you and the viewer will respond to them. *642* was made the day after my visit to Oradour-sur-Glane in France. I was so moved by the story behind the deserted village, where the 642 residents were rounded up by the Nazis in June 1944 and then systematically murdered within a few hours, with only two escaping. I used the colours of the French flag within the piece and, without the explanation I have given, the number on the piece might be meaningless, but it was important to me to stitch out my thoughts in recognition of the souls who were lost.

Money Worries

The quilt artwork illustrated here is a very personal piece of work that uses extracts from my maternal grandmother's diaries. She was a farmer's wife and there was never much money around. The diaries catalogue her concerns with profit and loss and the price of things. At the back of the diary there are numerous 'sums' which were usually her totals for egg sales that she made from the kitchen door and to local shop keepers. My grandmother's handwriting is very familiar to me and so it seemed only right to try to capture that exactly. I did this by photocopying the diary entry and enlarging it slightly. I then placed the photocopy over a sheet of typewriter carbon paper and traced the words on to the quilt top. I had to press quite hard to get the marks to come through on the coverlet and you might find the same if your quilt top is very quilted and lumpy. Practise on a separate section first to see if it is going to work. If the lettering is not coming through then it is because your carbon paper is not fresh or you need a flatter surface than a quilt. It could be a piece of linen, for example.

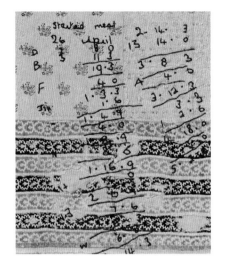

I was now ready to stitch. I chose a red perle thread and decided to use couching as my technique as I felt that it would allow me to capture the curviness of the handwriting. I worked one letter at a time, bringing the needle and thread out and then using my finger to lay out the shape on the top. I then pushed the needle back in and came up and couched, putting an overstitch over the top of the shaped thread. Most letters could not be done in one action and needed part couching and part straight stitch. This might sound difficult and you do need to practise before you start the project, but you will be surprised at how you pick up speed and how easily you can form the letters using this method.

This may seem ambitious to some of you but at least have a try at doing your own initials on a scrap of fabric so that you can sign off your own textile work when you finish something.

Above (detail) and below: *Money Worries*, 2016, 103 x 45cm (40½ x 17¾in). Lettering using couching and backstitch on to antique coverlet.

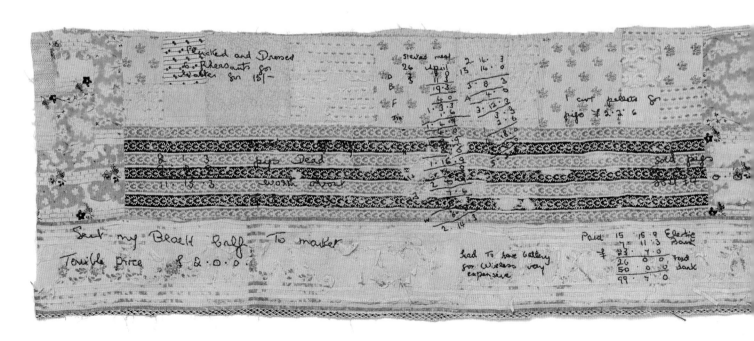

Appliqué

Appliqué is the application of one fabric on to another. It is a broad term that can describe a range of techniques and approaches. There is an historical tradition of combining appliqué with quilting stitches and embroidery, Baltimore Album Quilts being the best example. Appliqué can be decorative, can tell a story and, in the past, was an inclusive technique with perhaps many women making their own appliqué blocks and then joining them together. I keep with the traditional ways and mostly use the finger-turned appliqué technique within my own work as it suits the more folk-art-style narrative I am trying to achieve.

The method I use is to plan the design and make templates out of card for all the components. You then draw round a template on the back of your fabric, add a 6mm (¼in) allowance for turning (or construct a template that includes the turn allowance) and cut the shape out. Pin your motif to the base fabric or bit of quilt and then use ordinary sewing thread and slipstitch to apply it, tucking the edge under as you go. You can work from a ready-made design or draw your own. I will demonstrate this a little more by talking you through a personal appliqué project.

Staffordshire animal ornaments

My daughter, Alice Pattullo, who is an illustrator, and I share a love for collecting from flea markets. For me, it is mostly textiles but both of us love folk art and pottery and cannot resist a china figurine of a bird or, if we can find them at a reasonable price, a pair of what are traditionally called 'wally' dogs. In Victorian and Edwardian times thousands of homes would have had these Staffordshire figurines of dogs, usually spaniels, on their mantlepieces. Staffordshire is a county of England and was home to many potteries including Wedgwood, Spode and Royal Doulton. These chinaware factories would have produced the original figurines using what is known as a press mould, but since then Staffordshireware has been heavily reproduced using the newer method of slip moulding. The animal figurines you pick up at a market may be old but they are almost certainly a reproduction. Alice has made drawings of some of the ornaments that she has collected and they have formed a basis for her screen prints. Her drawings have in turn inspired me to create a collection of finger-turned appliqués. If you want to have a go, you could try following the method I describe here for building up a picture of a pair of spaniels.

1 First of all, do your research. Many breeds of dogs, cats, cows, sheep, deer and other animals were popular as figurines. Collect images from books and the internet and visit museum collections so that you can make an informed and inspired decision as to what you are going to portray.

2 Find a background fabric. I was lucky to be able to source a lovely old tumbling-block patchwork quilt, but you could use a piece of blanket, a more contemporary quilt top, or a sturdy piece of furnishing fabric. Most of the china figurines were predominantly white so I think it is important to choose something that is dark to provide a contrast. Even a piece of wool felt would do.

Above: *Wally Dogs*,
2017, 45 x 40cm
(18 x 16in). Appliqué
and hand stitching
on tumbling-block
quilt section.

Left: Alice Pattullo,
2017. Screenprint.

Above: *Dalmations*,
2017, 45 x 40cm
(18 x 16in). Appliqué
and hand stitching
on tumbling-block
quilt section.

Right: Cats, 2017,
45 x 40cm
(18 x 16in). Appliqué
and hand stitching
on tumbling-block
quilt section.

3 Analyze your subject matter and try to break it down into sections. It might be easiest to do the ears, the legs and the tail as separate elements layered on to a basic appliquéd shape. The shapes I have drawn here can be enlarged on a photocopier and could be adapted into a cat or dog. Your work will be much more interesting if you create your own design. I have to fiddle around for ages with the sizes of my templates, laying them on to the background until I get a size and composition I am happy with. I have chosen to work with the traditional mantelpiece pairs but many single ornaments were also produced.

Enlarge templates up to size needed. Add ears, legs and tails as separate elements.

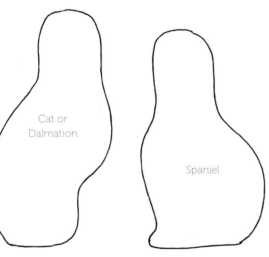

Cat or Dalmation

Spaniel

4 Select the fabric for your animal. This is where you need to consider your background in relation to the appliqué. Most of the figurines of dogs and cats have a lot of white in them so will show up best against a dark background. I would normally say use a selection of patchwork-type cottons for appliqué, and these are easiest to use, but here I have used the reverse side of some old curtain material. I like the way you can just see other colours coming through. The material is not stiff and new but has been washed many times so is soft enough to be able to turn the edges.

5 Pin the main body template on to the back of your fabric and then cut out allowing an extra 6mm (¼in) all the way round. Notch any tight curves.

6 Pin the fabric to your foundation. I do not tack or pin down the turn but just get going. Turn the edge under 6mm (¼in) with your finger or needle just ahead of where you are going to sew and then sew down with a tiny slipstitch. Once you have got a few stitches in this is very easy. If you come to a difficult curve where you need to ease the fabric then maybe notch a little more to get it to go round the curve. Layer up the other pieces using the same technique. Details of markings on the body have been overlaid with further appliquéd fabrics, sometimes turning the edge under, but also leaving raw edges to appear more naturalistic.

7 For the embroidery, I return to my imagery to see how the face and fur have been depicted and try to express this through my stitching. Couching, stem stitch, French knots and chain stitch have been used. I have tried to remain true to the original pottery design so some of the features may appear naïve but I aim to keep them looking authentic.

Bags

I have always been interested in bags found in museums but they are usually highly decorative, precious, and are there because they have been valued and preserved. You rarely see examples of bags used by the poorer classes, as they were made of less sophisticated materials, were used regularly, wore out and were not kept. I have a lovely collection of bags, some of them from my own family, that were used to hold papers, coins, handkerchiefs and stockings.

In an era when we are becoming more aware of the danger that discarded plastic is having on our environment and we are no longer offered free plastic bags when we go shopping, it is good to see that more people are using cloth bags. For many years I used a lot of sealable plastic bags in my studio to store different projects, but recently I have tried to eradicate plastic from my workspace and have endeavoured to make multi-functional bags from

Left: Tablet pouch, 2015, 13.5 x 18cm (5¼ x 7in).

Right: Mandy James, *Log Cabin Messenger Bag*, 2019, 24 x 27cm (9½ x 10½in). Made from an old quilt with a lining of French floral fabric. Strap in heavyweight gingham and hand-stitched with linen thread.

fabric and zips I already have or from pieces of old quilt. My Kindle nestles inside a little bag made from a segment of an Irish quilt, my iPad is also protected by a thick quilt sleeve, and I make numerous pouch bags of different sizes out of furnishing-fabric samples to keep needlework tools in and for sewing projects that I want to carry around and work with on the go. The ones I have made for myself give me great joy and I have also made them for friends. They do get a bit grubby and because they are made from an old fabric they have a limited life, but they can be repaired and darned and re-patched. I have never seen an antique bag made from a piece of quilt (there are plenty of contemporary examples) but this does not mean that resourceful women did not recycle their quilts into receptacles – just that they were never photographed or preserved.

It is easy to make a bag by simply folding a piece of quilt so that you have a pocket and a flap, as I have done for the tablet case (shown left), or use just a section of a quilt within the construction as Mandy James has done with her messenger bag (above).

I would like to share my favourite way of making a bag which is a little more labour intensive but turns my familiar textile collage techniques into something a bit more functional. Most of these bags have an element of a piece of fabric unpicked from a quilt mixed in with other fabrics, often vintage. This is important: do not go out and buy fabrics for this project, tempting as it may be – use what you already have.

Making a collaged pouch bag

1 First of all, I think about what I am going to put in the pouch and then make the bag big enough to hold it. I play about with bits of folded paper till I get the right size. I then draw round this paper template on to a piece of bonded curtain lining or cotton quilt batting. You could use a piece of blanket, wool felt or wadding as an alternative. We will call this the base fabric. When cut out and folded it will be the exact size of the pouch bag.

2 Next, I gather my fabrics, often including pieces of quilt. I always have a colour story which might be led by one of the pieces of fabric or a postcard image. The French artist Pierre Bonnard is a good one to look at for interesting colour combinations. For this project I do not want to use a thick piece of quilt in combination with other thinner materials so I usually unpick the top layer of a quilt, particularly a wholecloth quilt or a French boutis (trapunto) quilt or I use just the top of a coverlet.

3 I pin the fabrics onto the 'fuzzy' side of the curtain lining. I have a 1–2cm (³/₈–³/₄in) overhang around the outside edge that will eventually be turned in. I frequently fold to the purse shape so that I can see what is going to

Left: The left-hand image shows fabrics pinned on the base fabric with a 2cm (¾in) overhang. On the right you can see the back with the fabrics attached and embroidered, the overhang slip stitched into place, and the lining partially stitched in.

happen at the front, as I do not want the front flap to obscure something really interesting. When it comes to sewing the pieces down, I leave the edges raw and unturned as that is how I like it, but you could piece it together on a machine or finger turn all the edges if that is what you prefer. I use my usual stab stitch or overcast stitch to attach my pieces of fabric.

4 Now I turn the whole piece over and wrap the edges round the base lining and sew down. This can just be a tacking stitch, as it will be covered by the lining, but try to ensure it sinks into the base fabric and does not show on the right side. I now add any decorative hand stitching that I want to the surface collage. I use just a few stitches but you could use more if you wish. Next choose a lining fabric and attach using slipstitch over the inside turned edges.

5 To make the purse or bag, fold into shape as required and stitch up the sides with an overcast stitch. I sometimes make a feature of this using big stitches and a perle thread. You can use a decorative stitch such as buttonhole, cross stitch or herringbone.

6 You next need to consider how the bag will close. You could attach poppers, or hook-and-loop tape, or create a buttonhole by hand or on the machine. I like to use a detached buttonhole stitch over two strands of thread to make a looped closure. It is a bit fiddly; use a thick cotton thread, perle or coton à broder rather than a stranded embroidery thread for this.

Right: Three hand-stitched pouch bags. Average size 15 x 13cm (5½ x 6in). Recycled fabrics, including quilt unpickings, attached to a base fabric, folded and hand stitched up the side.

Stitching on Quilts

A quilt necessarily contains stitches as they are what hold the three layers together. The stitches might be utilitarian but often the quilting can be highly decorative and planned with feathers, leaves, flowers, scrolls and knots. I live and work in the north-east of England, which has a strong local tradition of beautifully worked wholecloth quilts. Pattern templates would be handed down through families and the women and men who drew the designs on to the top cloth, usually with a blue pencil, were called stampers. Two of the most famous from my region were Elizabeth Sanderson of Allenheads and Joe Hedley, who lived just along the valley from my studio and was brutally murdered, possibly for his quilting money. It is rare to find embroidered quilts, apart from within the redwork and crazy-quilt tradition, but I love to embroider on to the quilt or coverlet surface as I do not need to use a hoop, and the stitches I make further quilt the piece. It brings together my love of quilts and my love of embroidery and I like to stitch alongside and in counterpoint to someone else's handiwork.

I rarely have an embroidery design planned when I start a project. Instead, they are led by the collage pieces or the colours of the background patchwork. I attach the collage elements, if I am using them, in the usual way with a little overcast stitch, and then one of the most important decisions I have to make is the colour of the threads with which I am going to embroider. I look very carefully at the quilt top and collage elements for guidance as to where to start. In *Buds*, a collage and stitched drawing on a Victorian log-cabin block, the satin-stitched buds echo the rosebud shape as well as its colour. In *Suzani* a fragment of disintegrating Turkish embroidery has been embedded and merged into the surface of the quilt through the colour and shape of the stitches. They move in the same direction and have the same spatial relationship to each other as the original embroidery. In *Purple Flower* the loosely embroidered flower shapes have been suggested

Left: *Suzani* (top),
2019, 18 x 18cm
(7 x 7in). *Buds*
(middle) 2019,
14 x 14cm
(5½ x 5½in).
Purple Flower
(bottom), 2019,
13 x 21cm (5 x 8in).

Above: Crazy
quilt. Mixed fabrics,
including silks, and
hand stitching.
Collection of Jen
Jones, The Welsh
Quilt Centre.

Left: *Circle Flowers*,
2019, 30 x 21cm
(12 x 8¼in).
Embroidery
on Victorian
tumbling-block
quilt fragment.

by the motif on the fabric in the middle of the piece. The stitches are meant to convey the same fragility as that worn fabric, which was in fact unpicked from another quilt. The back of a quilt was used for this piece, although a little of the front was cut off and reassembled at the bottom to tell this story.

My advice would be to marry a piece of antique quilt with a few collaged fabrics you absolutely adore and these will inspire you to take an unchartered journey into stitching on to the quilt surface with, hopefully, pleasing transformational results.

We sometimes become so bent on learning a stitch or giving it a name that we forget to look at the shape it creates and the potential for pattern making. Stitchers from the 1950s and 1960s, such as Winsome Douglass, were great at recognizing the potential for combining stitches to create borders and patterns. In *Circle Flowers* I have taken inspiration from my old collection of embroidery books and have attempted to 'draw' the stylized circular flowers using simple and traditional stitches on top of a Victorian tumbling-block quilt. I encourage you not to over-plan a project of this type, but just to start with the middle of a flower and work out in concentric circles using traditional stitches such as buttonhole stitch, fern stitch, cross stitch, backstitch, running stitch, chain and detached chain stitch, French knots and stem stitch. When you feel you have enough flowers then you can think about the stems. I have used stem stitch but you could use chain stitch, couching or backstitch instead. Interestingly, it also echoes the beautiful quilt from The Jen Jones Collection on page 43. The quilt was from a farmhouse in The Gower, in Wales, and was owned by the Griffiths family. The dates 1841–1902 in one of the panels suggest it was made to remember a loved one.

Cross Over

Folk Art design books and cross-stitch charts will give you clear diagrams to work from. I find it difficult to work from a pattern book and prefer to take a more freestyle approach as I have done in *Red Work*. In this case, I used a piece of quilt that was too thick and layered – it probably had a blanket inside, so it was difficult to stitch all the way through the layers. I persisted, but I encourage you to learn from my mistake and choose a surface that is more pliable or it really will become work rather than a pleasure. Most of the old domestic embroidery will have been done from a pattern or transfer and you can use a piece of actual embroidery as a guide rather than the original pattern instructions. In *Wool Flowers* I really analyzed the original embroidery before I crossed over the design on to the quilt surface. I noted those little satin-stitch wiggles in the centre of the flowers, the inclusion of a few French knots and then the more open satin-stitch pattern making, working from inner to outer petals. I kept the piece on my desk as I was working to refer to, but I wanted to create something that was mine rather than copying someone else's design, so although it inspired me it is also considerably altered. For this project I chose a particularly worn piece of quilt and I roughed it up a bit more with a seam ripper before I started as I wanted to create a surface that the stitches really sank into.

Above (detail) and below: *Red Work*, 2018. Cross stitch on quilt fragment.

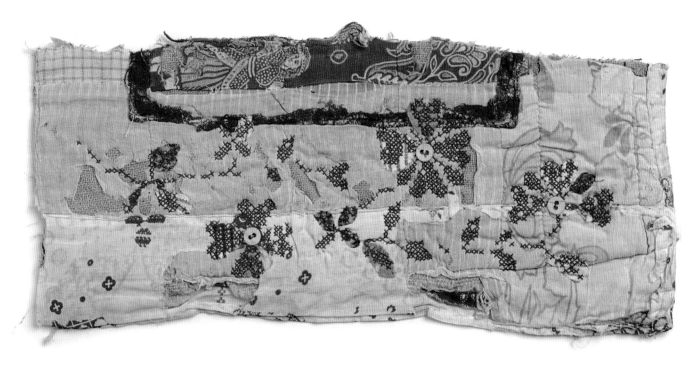

Above: *Wool
Flowers*, 2019,
28 x 30cm
(11 x 12in). Wool
embroidery on
very dilapidated
quilt surface.

Left: An
embroidered
table runner found
in a French market.
I used this as a
pattern reference
to work the
piece above.

Left: *Walk to the
Allotment*, 2019,
39 x 29cm
(15¼ x 11½in).
Appliqué and
wool embroidery
on quilt surface.

Tell a Story

Use your imagination and stitch imagery to convey a
personal story. This could be about your family, home,
a journey, an incident. My piece *Walk to the Allotment* is
not as accurate as a map but it is about my almost-daily
walk, over the railway line, through the cemetery and past
the community orchard to the site of my allotment. I drew
round the piece of quilt before I started and used a piece
of paper exactly the same size to plan out what I wanted to
include. I mapped out the main areas with a bright-coloured
tacking line before I started so I knew that I could fit the
main elements in. This piece of work developed over time
and the thinking time was just as important as the making
process. I kept thinking of things I wanted to include and
made notes all the time but also re-evaluated and took
things out. A piece like this can be concocted with very
simple stitches and though I had a simple drawing plan
to work from, I made the stitches up as I went along.
I intentionally wanted the work to look naïve and was
much influenced by looking at the work of Welsh stitcher
Primmy Chorley, who uses stitch to keep a record of the
events and emotions of her life.

CHAPTER TWO

Wool Work

Wool has been utilized by humankind since the Stone Age and is a natural, biodegradable product that comes from a sustainable source. In many countries sheep farming is part of the heritage and the fleeces shorn from the sheep each year have contributed to the manufacture of beautiful knitwear, woven fabrics such as Harris Tweed and spun wool for knitting and sewing. Inspirational wool embroidery can be found across many cultures, and ranges from simple Folk Art style stitching used as decoration on garments and domestic items, to the sophisticated production of crewel work popular in the 17th century.

You may have inherited old wool bed blankets, have knitwear that needs revitalizing or have found more interesting second-hand wool items such as the vintage wool dressing gown I have embroidered with flowers, or an old tweed or wool skirt that you can cut up. All of these can be embellished and transformed using wool yarn. Tapestry and embroidery yarns and knitting wool can be easily sourced second hand, so wool work can be a very economical as well as sustainable textile craft.

Left: Detail of wool embroidery on a gentleman's dressing gown.

Crewel Work

If you have something you want to transform with wool stitching and are unfamiliar with stitch types, then take a look at crewel-work embroidery for motif ideas and interesting stitches, particularly filling stitches.

Crewel work has been around for a thousand years and some would argue the Bayeaux Tapestry uses this technique. It is the working of stitches with wool on to a linen or wool fabric, usually with a specific type of 2-ply wool that can be separated into strands if needed. Crewel work was at its height from the mid-17th to mid-18th centuries but it was certainly an important inspiration for Morris and Company's popular textile designs. The Royal School of Needlework continues the good work of

disseminating this style of embroidery to the highest level from its department at Hampton Court Palace. In Jacobean times, it was used to decorate bed hangings and coverlets, curtains, garments and even bags and shoes. The designs of this time were very distinctive with stylized flowers, fruits, leaves and curving stems. There were also animals and mythical beasts such as unicorns and griffins. I have no urge to copy these patterns (but if you do there are many kits available) but like to use them as a starting point. I love to look at books on crewel embroidery that have clear black-and-white drawings of the designs and from these I will extract elements such as a leaf shape or a flower head and draw my own. Even then these drawings are just a guide and I rarely copy them exactly when I am stitching.

Left: *Lattice Flowers*, 2019, 30 x 26cm (12 x 10in). Wool embroidery on a 20th-century crazy quilt and inspired by crewel-work designs. The piece has been bound with an edging that was the original fabric on the back of the quilt.

Crewel work is needlework for an embroiderer with a good knowledge of basic stitches or a willingness to learn them. Stitches that are typically used are satin stitch, couching, stem stitch, long-and-short stitch, fishbone stitch and split stitch, but there are many more. They are often used to interlace with each other, building up what are known as composite stitches. Another way to recognize crewel embroidery is through the use of filling stitches which are an effective way to block in a large shape.

It is worth making a set of stitch samples with wool, as I have done, so you can see the effects that you can get. In true crewel embroidery a single strand is used for a touch of delicacy and a thick or even doubled strand used for greater impact, but I do not limit myself to just crewel wool and use whatever I have, so sometimes it is tapestry wool or even knitting wool. In my stylized crewel-work-influenced piece I have transformed a rather ugly crazy-quilt top which did contain some wool fabrics but also bits of synthetic fleece and blanket. You could create your own patchwork to work on or try working the stitches on to a garment such as an old tweed jacket.

Right: Crewel-work stitch samples.

Blankets

Wool blankets are easily found second hand or might be inherited. Most of us do not use them as part of our bedding these days but they can be reduced in size to make throws or cushions and can be refreshed with embroidery on a corner or edge. Sometimes it is even enough to use a contrasting colour of thread to buttonhole stitch round the edge where you have cut. You can work with an embroidery thread, but you may find that it sinks into the pile, so as a general rule always use a tapestry or crewel wool for your embroidery. Stretch the section you are working on into an embroidery hoop before you start stitching to avoid any tension problems.

I particularly love blankets that have a striped edge and working this in as part of the design. The pieces illustrated here show two very different approaches. In the floral sample I have worked organically out from the centre of each flower with straight stitches, making it up as I went along. The other example uses the stripes as a guideline for a cross-stitch pattern which uses the colour story of the bullfinch tapestry fragment. I made this Penelope

Below: Wool stitching on the edge of a blanket.

tapestry kit piece as a child. It was proudly framed in a white plastic frame and the edges glued under with Copydex. I found it when clearing out my parents' loft and it was good to revisit it and include it rather than throwing it away. The cross stitch is personally significant as my mother did kits like this all her life. A piece of found wool embroidery such as this might be a good starting point to give you a colour palette to work with and the motifs might suggest design ideas of your own. Attach it with wool thread to your blanket.

Above: *Bullfinch*, 2019, 33 x 25cm (13 x 10in). Found needlepoint with cross stitch embroidery.

Sailors' Wool Work

In many British museums you will be able to see examples of wool work pictures made by sailors. Compton Verney Art Gallery holds some fine examples in its Folk Art collection. The making of these wool-work pictures was at its height from about 1840 to the beginning of World War I. Sailors were happy to turn to a time-absorbing craft on long voyages. The pieces are usually stitched in long filling stitches but sometimes other decorative stitches were also used. Sailors would have had to know how to sew in order to mend their clothes, nets and sails on board, and there is evidence that there was such a craze for the craft that many seamen continued stitching in retirement on dry land. These pictures are naïve and nearly always show a ship but there are also pictures depicting landscapes, quayside farewells, whales, and often flags and other patriotic symbols were incorporated. They are wonderful to look at and you can perhaps extract ideas from them to incorporate in your own work or to upcycle a garment and give it a nautical theme.

I have worked in wool too, but rather than make a picture, I have transformed a friend's very shrunken jumper. I am interested in the way sailors so often cling to superstitions, and so my inspiration was a screen print by my daughter, who has extensively researched the subject.

I have worked with crewel wools in bright colours like the original sewing sailors did. If you are doing a project like this, it is very important to plan it first. I made a paper template of the actual size of the jumper and then drew my ideas on to this so I knew how it would look before I started. From the paper drawings, I was able to make a template of the seagull which I drew round, with tailors' chalk, on to the navy blue jumper. I have used mostly long-and-short stitch which was the most common stitch used in the sailors' pictures. The superstition – the seagull bears the soul of a drowned sailor – is embroidered along the bottom. This was an adult's jumper but can now be worn by a three year old!

Colin Millington

Above: Colin
Millington,
The Lost Whale,
2018, 54 x 48cm
(21¼ x 19in).
Wool and synthetic
wool on calico.

Left: *The Seagull*,
2019. Wool
embroidery
on shrunken
wool sweater.

Colin Millington, born 1936, is a retired sailor who lives in
Sheringham in Norfolk. He makes wool works inspired by
the 19th century 'woolies' while bringing a bit of his own
individual style to each project. He initially started with
copying old pictures but is now confident at coming up with
his own designs and has developed a visual language which
is unique while referencing the past. Perspective and scale
might not be quite accurate but this all adds to the charm.
Millington works with 2-ply wool, often sourced from charity
shops, on calico that is attached to stretchers. He mostly
uses long-and-short filling stitch, but, like the original sailor
stitchers, he sometimes resorts to other stitches such as
chain stitch or backstitch for linear effects. He is represented
by Paffron and Scott (www.paffronandscott.co.uk).

Yllebroderier

Yllebroderier is the Swedish word for wool embroidery. I fell in love with this style of stitching after visiting Sweden. In the Nordiska Museet in Stockholm and the Dalarnas Museum in Falun I saw inspiring examples of the way woven clothing and household items had been made beautiful through the use of imaginative embroidery. The early examples of embroidery often contained imagery related to Swedish legends as well as biblical figures. Flowers and trees (symbolizing life) were the most common motif but there were also many fine examples of narrative pictures featuring stylized figures and animals. The stitching was worked with skill in gay colours obtained through dyeing with indigenous herbs, moss and vegetables. In Swedish museums there are often room sets of peasant and farmhouse homes, which show how brightly coloured cushions, pillows, bedcovers and hangings enhanced interiors. Embroidery was not limited to inside the house and the Nordiska Museet has some fine examples of carriage and sleigh cushions, many of which were made in Skåne.

There is much that we can take from the study of embroidered folk textiles from other cultures. I urge you, however, to make your work original by doing your own research, drawing, and then coming up with your own designs.

Making an *Yllebroderier*

1 Research. Collect together images, make drawings and immerse yourself in the world of Swedish wool embroidery through reading books or using resources like Pinterest or Google image searches.

2 Start to make drawings of elements that you like and observe closely the type of stitching used. You might want to make notes of this next to your drawings. Try to work up a few designs using the different elements that you have drawn. Draw, or trace, to the size you might want to embroider and then from this trace off the silhouette and make templates. You can move these around on the cloth you are going to embroider to help with the placement of the design.

3 The traditional embroidery of Sweden was usually worked on to hand-woven linen or wool. This can be expensive, so look for second-hand wool skirts, jackets or offcuts as I have done in my designs, where I have worked on to an old red wool skirt from a charity shop and, as shown in the photograph above, on to a piece of navy blue wool fabric, also recycled.

4 Draw round your templates with tailors' chalk if your foundation fabric is dark, or use a water-soluble pen on lighter fabrics. If you are working fairly intensively then the chalk could disappear quite quickly, so you might like to go round the silhouette with a tacking stitch that you can remove as you go along. On the red skirt I have taken a shortcut by drawing some of my templates on to a wool felt fabric which I have appliquéd on and then embroidered over.

5 Choose a range of wool threads to work with. You might have coloured up your design but I prefer to work instinctively with a small range of, say, eight colours. Start with the easiest part of the design and decide whether you are going to outline the motif with, for example, stem stitch or backstitch, or just start filling in the shape with long-and-short stitch, which is the most common stitch used in this type of embroidery. In *Folk Lady* I started with an outline of the skirt and then moved on to filling it in. You may need to work with your fabric in a hoop or frame to keep it taught. In whatever I do I try to remain flexible, so I am quite willing to veer from my original plans and to add new elements. I am sure this is how the original wool works were developed as they have a quirkiness and vitality that suggests they evolved as the needleworker went along. If you feel you cannot do this then you could always use a kit.

You can have the finished piece stretched and framed, make it into a cushion or put another piece of fabric (felt is good) on the back and attach rings in the corner to hang directly on the wall. If you have worked on to a garment which you are going to wear, such as my red skirt with the horse, then wash it with great care following guidelines for washing wool, or only wear for special occasions.

Left: Old red wool skirt with wool felt appliquéd horse and wool embroidery, 2019.

Canvas Works

Howard Carter, the famous discoverer of the tomb of
Tutankhamun, found what is probably the earliest example
of needlepoint. Diagonal stitches were often used by the
Egyptians to sew up their canvas tents which is why the
main worked stitch in needlepoint is called tent stitch.
Embroidery on linen has been done for centuries, but the
needlepoint that we know today probably evolved with
the development of steel needles which allowed people
to emulate woven tapestries through close stitching on
canvas. This is why in the UK needlepoint is sometimes
known as canvas work or tapestry. Needlepoint is always
worked on a canvas mesh and, though there are a range
of needlepoint stitches, most needlepoint is worked in tent
stitch. If it is worked on a very fine canvas then it is known
as petit point. Berlin wool work is slightly different
in that it is usually worked in cross stitch with wool.

Early needlepoint was fine work done by ladies of leisure,
including Marie Antoinette, Mary Queen of Scots and
Elizabeth I. Eventually needlepoint became more accessible
to the middle classes through the availability of mass-
produced patterns for the European and American markets.
The patterns would often take their inspiration from the
natural world, historical sources and other cultures. The
Victorians had a penchant for animals and flowers and
contemporary designers of wool work, such as Elizabeth
Bradley, don't stray too far from the tastes of the past. I love
floral needlepoint and sections often creep into my textile
collages combined with bits of quilt and other fabrics.

Right: *Purple Rose,*
2019, 30 x 45cm
(12 x 17¾in).
Embroidered
patchwork of
vintage fabric
scraps incorporating
needlepoint motifs.

Using Needlepoint

You might be lucky and discover your needlepoint in a finished state, blocked and framed up, but it is more likely you will find a printed canvas that has not been stitched at all or a half-finished kit. You can work with all of these in different ways but if you have a choice, always go for something which has been printed on to a good-quality linen canvas rather than a cheap white one that can be rough on the hands and difficult to use. If you have areas of open canvas where there is no stitching then you might have to consider putting a backing fabric behind so the light does not show through. You may also encounter problems with an irregular shape as, unless the needlepoint has been worked by a very careful stitcher, the piece may be pulled and distorted. I just accept this, but you will find instructions about 'blocking' in instruction books for needlepoint and, through that method, you may be able to rescue the shape.

Your needlepoint might be filthy, particularly if it has been used as a cushion cover. I would, in that case, wash the piece very gently in barely warm water with soap flakes or a product for washing special woollens. Change the water frequently and do not rub the piece or wring it but rather swish it up and down in the water. At the end of the washing process you can get rid of some of the excess water by using a clean sponge to soak up the extra moisture. I would suggest detaching any fabric, such as backing fabric for a cushion, in case it is not colour-fast.

You now need to decide if you are going to use the whole canvas-work picture, finished or not, or cut into it. There is nothing wrong with cutting into the canvas but you are obviously going to be cutting through stitches which makes the stitching vulnerable to fraying. You cannot totally avoid this, but use plenty of close stitches when you appliqué and I advise using wool threads that are in keeping with the original textile.

You can:

- Use your needlepoint to make something useful such as a cushion cover, bag or even a coverlet.

- Join lots of found pieces together to make a patchwork.

- Appliqué the artwork on to a garment such as the pocket of a jacket or a skirt panel.

- Use the whole or part of a piece in a collage with other fabrics.

- If the original worked image is truly awful, consider turning it over and using the back to create a background texture to some appliqué, or even embroider into it.

- Stitch over or unpick areas.

- Appliqué on to the canvas or stitched areas.

Garments

Below: Skirt made
from an old quilt
with appliquéd
needlepoint
flowers, 2018.

If you are going to use needlepoint to embellish a garment you really need to turn the edges to make it durable. This is almost impossible unless you are using the whole piece and an unworked canvas edge is there for you to turn in. Most of the garments I make or decorate are not functional and designed to hang on the wall as part of the styling of a room so this does not apply. However, I am sensitive to how I attach the needlepoint and try to use a tapestry or crewel wool that's in keeping with the canvas work. The skirt shown here was made from a tailor's sample quilt, retro rather than antique. The wadding was creeping out of the quilt so the bottom edge was bound to hide this. The skirt is embellished with nasturtium flowers taken from a needlepoint table runner. These have been attached with a little overcast stitch using a wool thread.

Kit Designs

Most needlepoint that you find second hand will have been designed by someone else. If you are lucky you will find a piece of finished 'tapestry' that has been designed well by one of the accomplished artists, such as Raymond Honeyman or Kaffe Fassett, who both work for Hugh Ehrman's kit company. However, much of what you find will be of poorer design, using garish colours. In my childhood I would receive a Penelope tapestry kit every Christmas. These came in a cardboard box with a picture of the finished object on the front and included the threads and a plastic frame. There was a crudeness about the designs but it is still the vintage Penelope tapestry pictures that appeal to me with their designs of a 'chocolate box' England and

their attempted reproductions of great paintings. I enjoy the challenge of trying to incorporate some of them into my work, and though I recognize that many hours have been spent on working them up, I feel no guilt at cutting into them.

In the example shown above I have used a kitsch needlepoint of a thatched cottage and garden and continued the bright colours out into the framing using a section of a 1970s synthetic quilt. It was a real challenge for me to use this fabric! In order to support the thin cloth I had to attach this framing to a piece of felt to make it the same thickness as the tapestry it encloses. I have worked into the garden with more appliquéd flowers and stitching.

Left: *Summer*, 2019, 40 x 50cm (15¾ x 19½in). An embroidered tapestry kit given a new lease of life with the addition of appliqué, stitching and a patchwork border.

Right (detail) and below: *Fleurs d'après Brueghel*, 2018. Unfinished needlepoint canvas, still in its stretcher, with appliquéd and embroidered additions.

One option is to finish the work and then remove it from the frame, 'block' it if it has distorted and make it up into a cushion, a piece of upholstery or wall art. I have found these unfinished framed tapestry kits a good starting point for the application of other materials and the frame can become part of the finished artwork. In fact, I like best of all when the manufacturer's name and the colour grid is still showing at the side. I cannot pretend that it is easy to work within the frame unless you have a frame stand, but I like the challenge of bringing other fabrics on to the top of the wool picture as I have shown in *Fleurs d'après Brueghel*. I attached the fabrics on to the top of the needlepoint canvas using the finger-turned appliqué technique.

Ulla-Stina Wikander

Below: Ulla-Stina
Wikander, *Vacuum
Cleaner*, 2013.
Mixed media.

Opposite: Ulla-Stina
Wikander, *Iron Lady*,
2016. Mixed media.

Ulla-Stina is an artist based in Stockholm/Kullavik, Sweden. For many years she has collected cross stitch and needlepoint embroidery from flea markets and vintage shops. She gives these often kitsch and whimsical pieces, which were sewn by women in domestic settings, a new life by covering and combining them with other discarded objects from the home. An electric mixer, a telephone, a vacuum cleaner are all transformed by the application of the textile surface, and once 'dressed up' we view the objects as art pieces rather than utilitarian products. With their colourful skins the objects can no longer fulfil their purpose but they have been given a new life.

Useful and Beautiful

It is always good to make something useful out of a treasured textile that no longer serves its original purpose. I sew every day, so it is important to me to surround myself with beautiful needlework sundries as they sit next to me in the studio, always in sight. I have a turned wood bowl for my pins, baskets for threads and many needlecases, including the one shown left and below, which utilizes some found fine wool stitching. I have joined two sections to create a cover, used wool felt pieces for the inside and sewn it together with pamphlet stitch. Pamphlet stitch is very easy and ideal for this purpose. Instructions are widely available online.

Above and below:
Needlecase with
needlepoint cover
and wool felt pages.

Ann Stephens

Ann Stephens uses the pieces of needlepoint she sources
to make needlework accessories. For the scissor case she
experimented first with folded paper to get the shape right
and to make sure the pockets were the right size for her
own scissors. She lined the pouch, attaching the edges with
a decorative buttonhole stitch and then stitched up the
middle to create two pockets. She has further decorated
the middle seam with French knots, feather stitch and boot
buttons. Ann lives in France in an area with many walnut
groves and, with much of her work, the last thing she does
is to dip the piece in a walnut bath to knock the colour
back. The little pincushion was made as a result of necessity
in a workshop and stuffed with tiny bits of fabric that were
lying around the room.

Left: *Pink Rose*, 2017, 13 x 26cm (5¼ x 10¼in). A piece of needlepoint has had its edges turned over and attached with a network of cross stitches in wool on to a section of a dressing gown.

Right: The reverse of a piece of tapestry, which has become felted in the wash, is embellished with, in one example, a satin stitch flower, and in the other, a grid of running stitches. All worked in wool.

The Back

I would encourage you to see what you can do with the back of old needlepoint pieces. I often find the imperfection of the back much more interesting than the regularity of the front. I like to see the workings on the back as threads criss-cross. You can further work into these with your own stitches, or use the back within a collage, integrating the piece into the foundation with your own stitching echoing what is going on. Here, in *Pink Rose* (shown left), cross stitches in similarly coloured wools have helped the rose blend into the dressing gown fragment. In the other examples, the stitching has been worked on to the back of a needlepoint canvas which has been washed and become slightly felted. I love the way the stitches sink into the texture of the background, which is, of course, helped by the selection of threads that echo the base fabric in terms of colour. The image on the front, which might not be to your taste, becomes unimportant and what is happening on the back is the starting point for your transformative stitching.

Left: A moth-eaten doll's coat was darned visibly to match the coat scarf.

Below: A tattered piece of quilt has been partially mended with freestyle darning in wool.

Darning

Darning is a technique that grew out of necessity. Darning, the closure of a hole with woven stitches, was used to extend the longevity of clothing and knitwear, and to repair treasured household items such as table linen and sheets. Darning can often be found on old woollen items that have been attacked by moths, a more prevalent problem in the past when houses were damper. Darning your own items, or preloved ones you have acquired, contributes to a sustainable lifestyle, encouraging us to keep items for longer rather than buying more and more. Darning is done using a thread similar in composition to the material of the items needing to be mended and as near as possible in colour. A good darn was meant to be almost invisible. Sometimes darning is combined with the application of a piece of fabric or patch.

In recent years there has been a revival in darning techniques and a new term, 'visible mending' invented for it. Artists such as Celia Pym and Tom of Holland have led the way in promoting the use of colourful yarns to draw attention to the mending rather than away. Think of darning as a decorative stitch and try using different coloured yarns for warp and weft, allow the stitching to be unfinished in some places or continue to decorate by spreading further than the area that has been darned.

Felt

Felt is one of the oldest examples of textiles, going back thousands of years. It is made through the use of pressing water (and sometimes soap) into wool, the friction creating a durable textile that can be shaped or sewn into a useful artefact. It has been made across many cultures and often combines functionality with decoration. For most of us, felting is something we associate with washing a treasured jumper on the wrong setting of the washing machine. There are many felt makers all over the world stretching the boundaries of this ancient process, not just using wool but combining with man-made fibres and hand dyeing. Ellie Langley, who is a shepherdess and felt maker living in the North Pennines, uses purely British wool gathered from her own herd of beloved sheep. She makes hats, lampshades and bags, but I particularly love her cozy slippers. I show below some examples of how you can transform and personalize slippers with wool embroidery. My slippers are handmade by Ellie but you could buy something similar and have a go. It is very important that you have a plan. Draw the front of the slipper to size and then design into that space on paper first. I do not mark the felt but just start in the middle and work outwards. The flowers shown here have been worked in tapestry wool and mostly utilize satin stitch.

Left: Felt slippers made by Ellie Langley have been embellished in wool embroidery worked by Mandy Pattullo.

CHAPTER THREE

Linen and Lace

You are probably reading this book because you are a textile hoarder. You might have kept embroidered pieces worked by your mother or another relative and will almost certainly have a bag of lace. Like me, you may regularly add to this collection by buying more cloth and lace in antique fairs and charity shops and, when abroad, cannot resist a length of old linen or silk or an example of a local textile technique. This chapter suggests ways to use those things we already have, get them out of the cupboard, and make our own mark on them by using them in a new context, stitching into them or working on to them with other fabric. I would like to help you transform your precious old stuff into contemporary heirlooms which will be treasured anew by a future generation.

Left: Detail of *Swedish Summer*, 2019 (see page 76).

Vintage Embroidery

In the past, when there were fewer pressures on time, people spent hours stitching on cloth to decorate their homes. The stitching was usually guided by a purchased transfer design or one that had come free with a magazine. These pieces should be treasured, but they do not fit easily into home decoration styles now, so using the nicest pieces to cut and reassemble into something new can be the best way of displaying them.

Most embroidery was floral, and I particularly love needlework where I am able to cut out individual motifs and then re-apply them to a new backing or a garment. The example shown below uses individual flower heads worked by many different people but gathered on to a woven table runner that I sourced in Sweden. The linen fabrics on to which the flowers were stitched are difficult to turn so the flowers have been attached using a simple overcast stitch. This means that the work won't withstand heavy use or washing but could be used as a table centrepiece for special occasions. I have embroidered the stems with a variety of stitches including stem stitch, feather stitch, backstitch, couching, whipped running stitch, wheatear and herringbone stitches. In the embellishment of the cricket trousers (shown opposite) a similar thing has been done, again cutting up tablecloths and tray cloths for flowers within a defined colour scheme. The trousers have been, in a sense, made useless through the addition of the found embroidered elements but they hang in my studio as an artwork and remind me of English cricket fields and cottage gardens at the height of summer.

Below: *Swedish Summer*, 2019, 65 x 21cm (25½ x 8¼in). A woven table runner sourced in Sweden is embellished with flowers cut from domestic embroidered items.

Right: A young man's cricket trousers have been customized with pretty needlework taken from embroidered charity-shop finds.

1

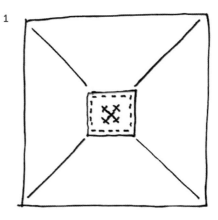

2

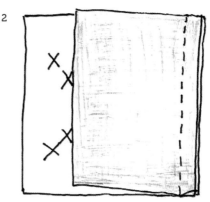

3

You could use your collection of vintage needlework to
make cushions and bags. A big item, such as a tablecloth,
can be made into a garment. Individual pieces can be
patched together to make coverlets and quilts. You could
just use sections in your patchwork, as I have done above,
in a log-cabin block. I have used a piece of cross stitch
but it could have been any piece of 'found' needlework.
Log cabin is usually worked with dark and light areas, to
suggest sunshine and shadow, around a central red square
suggesting the heart of the home, and can be quickly
made up by machine or hand. I have merely constructed
my block using fabrics I felt complemented the central
motif. It could be joined to others to make a bigger piece
or act as a background for appliqué or embroidery. If you
are making a one-off square, it is not so essential that the
strips are the same width, and, in fact, I own several antique
log-cabin quilts in which there is a lot of unevenness in the
measurements – this adds to their charm.

4

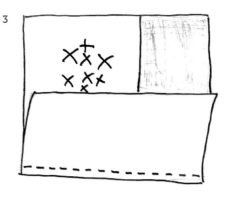

Left: *The Black Pot*, 2019,
36 x 24cm (14 x 9½in). A piece
of vintage embroidery has been
combined with an old piece of
log cabin in this textile collage.

Above: Log-cabin square
25 x 25cm (10 x 10in)
incorporating a piece
of cross stitch.

Handkerchief Art

Handkerchiefs are not so commonly used or carried now that we have access to more hygienic and convenient paper tissues. They were usually given as gifts at Christmas, often in multiples, packed flat in decorative boxes. Most people had cotton hankies with plain white for men and for women prints or plain colours and perhaps a bit of lace edging or a machine-embroidered motif. They are a vintage item that it is hard to find a new use for because the cloth itself is usually very fine, particularly if it has been washed a lot, so any stitch work you might apply needs to be worked with the handkerchief pulled tight in an embroidery hoop or with a lightweight interfacing ironed on to the back. I mostly use them as a background for stitched drawing and here I explain two different processes of working up pieces that relate to my own history.

Below: An oil painting of my birthplace inspired the stitched drawing on the handkerchief.

Handkerchief Homes

The naïve painting shows Hill Farm in Norfolk. I was born there, as was my mother, and the garden, which was mostly annual flowers grown from seed, was my grandmother's pride and joy. I have used a handkerchief in this instance as both a foundation fabric and a framing device. If you are making a portrait of your home, or a place you are fond of, then you could follow these steps.

How to make a handkerchief home portrait

1 Iron a lightweight interfacing on to the back of the handkerchief, following the manufacturer's instructions. This makes the handkerchief firmer to sew on.

2 Make sure your image fits into the central area of the handkerchief. You will almost certainly need to adjust the size of your image on a photocopier. Here, I have made the farm quite small as I knew that I wanted to make the garden and in particular the bowling green as important as the house.

3 Using tracing paper and pencil, trace off the main details of the building, bearing in mind that you will not be able to describe every brick in stitch. It is important, though, that you trace off the windows, door, chimneys. Doing this will give you an idea of what your stitched drawing will look like. If you are not happy with your tracing the first time then do it again, putting in more details like window frames and lintels. The amount of detail you can trace off will very much depend on the size of your image.

4 Now play about with the tracing to see where you want to put your image. I usually cut down the tracing paper so my image is enclosed in a smaller frame. I then cut a piece of typewriter or dressmaker's carbon paper to the same size and masking tape them to the hankie, carbon-ink side down, and the tracing over the top. Trace off the image lightly with a biro or sharp hard pencil. You could peel the papers back a little at the beginning to check the lines are coming through. They should be prominent enough to give you guidance with your sewing but not dark, thick and liable to smudge. Perhaps practise on another hankie first.

5 You are now ready to put the handkerchief in a hoop and start stitching. I use ordinary sewing threads and one or two strands of stranded embroidery thread. I work in backstitch and follow the outlines, now and then leaving a little breathing space to make it more interesting. You can use different coloured threads if you like.

6 If you want to add appliqué elements then be realistic and try to capture the mood of the garden by cutting out flowers from fabrics (Liberty prints work well) or use other embroidery stitches to describe the shapes of plants. I have simply used a little overcast stitch to appliqué these on, rather than turning the edges.

The example shown left is my current home which almost fills the fabric. I have not used a handkerchief here but a piece of damask table linen brought out at Christmas by my grandmother. The transfer of the image was done in the same way as for the handkerchief.

Left: *Home*, 2018.
Stitched drawing
on a tablecloth.

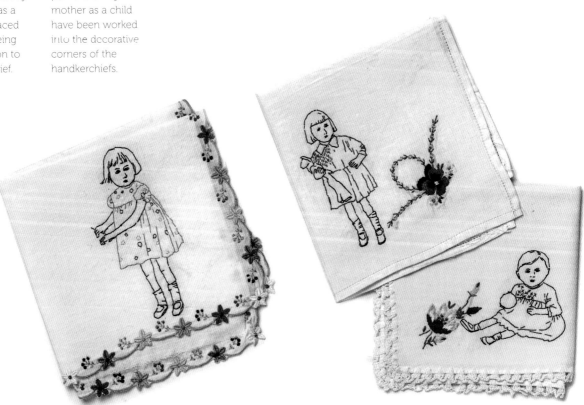

Handkerchief Portraits

For the stitched portraits of my mother as a child I have used a slightly different method to transfer the image. I have still traced off the main details from the original photograph but this time I have used a Frixion pen, a special pen with erasable ink. I taped the tracing behind the handkerchief and then taped the handkerchief to a light box so the image was visible beneath the cloth, then drew the image directly on to the handkerchief with the Frixion pen. If you do not have access to a light box, tape your hankie to a windowpane. When you have finished all your embroidery, the pen marks can be removed with a steam iron. In the last few years, there have been concerns about the marks coming back if the fabric is exposed to cold conditions such as being left in the boot of a car overnight or in the hold of an aeroplane, but if this happens, steam the lines out again. If you do not have a Frixion pen then a good alternative is a propelling pencil. I have not placed the image in the centre this time but have used the embroidered edge as a framing device. With these portraits I have brought in a little more colour through the use of decorative stitching, suggesting pattern and drawing attention to the clothing.

Above: The original photograph of my mother Jill, as a toddler, is traced off before being transferred on to a handkerchief.

Below: Three stitched portraits of my mother as a child have been worked into the decorative corners of the handkerchiefs.

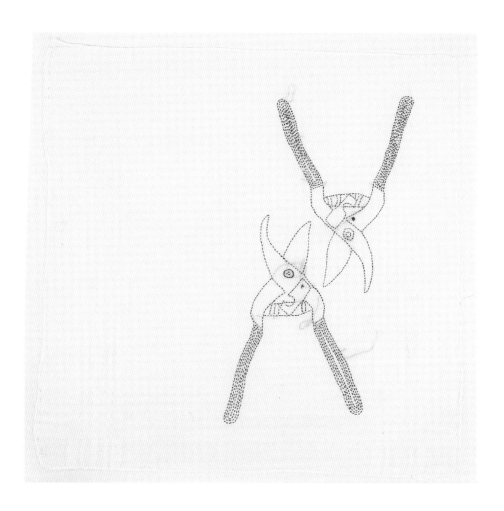

Below: Ruth Singer, *Tool Shed: Trowel*, 2012, 30cm (12in) square. Hand embroidery on old handkerchief.

Above: Ruth Singer, *Tool Shed: Secateurs*, 2012, 40cm (16in) square. Hand embroidery on old handkerchief.

Ruth Singer

Ruth Singer originally trained as a textile historian and her work in museums has fed into her fascination with objects and how they are preserved and displayed. She takes inspiration from often ordinary things, such as needlework tools, which nevertheless have a history of use and ownership, and transforms them with stitch techniques to create a new narrative. She collects, displays and curates these altered objects but sometimes the artwork she produces has personal resonance. Ruth's grandfather, who was a professional gardener from the age of 14, died in 2012. He was still growing vegetables aged 96 and left behind sheds full of beautifully maintained and well-used gardening tools. Ruth has used her grandfather's own handkerchiefs, found neatly ironed and folded in his airing cupboard, to stitch carefully observed studies of his tools and has effectively captured his love of gardening. These are personal pieces, but will speak to many who have had to clear houses and sheds after a bereavement or who use tools that have been passed down through the family.

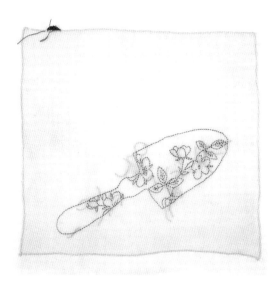

Cross Stitch

Cross-stitch pictures can, of course, be used in textile collages, either cut up or as the whole 'found' textile, but they can sometimes seem a bit twee. They can be saved and transformed by working into them a bit. *Duke* was a framed piece. I discarded the frame and extracted the cross stitch which had been laced and Sellotaped on to board. The stitching was extremely precise, but I needed to make the picture my own in some way, so I have painted into it to knock back the very white linen background. Sometimes a brush over with diluted black tea is enough but here I have used a bit more colour. If you want to do something similar, try following these steps, but be aware that the technique is a little uncontrollable!

Colouring the background might be enough for you but I could not resist collaging some scraps of my precious fabrics round the image, choosing them carefully to pick up the colours within the cross stitch. I have used the patchwork stars to suggest medals. They have been directly applied, using small overcast stitches, to the cross-stitch canvas. There is no backing fabric to my pieces and I hang them up with bulldog clips.

1 Make sure the cross stitch is absolutely flat by ironing out the creases where it has been wrapped round the board.

2 Place a large plastic sheet on a table and the cross stitch image-side up on top.

3 Analyze the design and work out which colours you might want to bring into the background and then mix up a number of Brusho paints in jam jars. Brusho is a non-toxic powder that you mix with water. It is a highly pigmented watercolour, not a dye, so you won't be able to wash your artwork afterwards as the colour will run out. Have a clean paintbrush for each jar and test each colour on a fabric similar to that of the background. I use decorating brushes as they give a broader sweep of colour.

4 Have a jam jar of water on standby and then start to apply colour to the background away from the image. If it seems too dark then quickly apply a water wash over the top. You are not using fabric paints so the Brusho will spread out in the same way as watercolour on paper. Use a second and third colour and allow them to mix and blend, and, as the colour moves nearer the image, let it bleed into the cross stitch a little.

5 Allow to dry naturally on the top of the plastic. If you move the fabric you risk moving the wet colour across the back of the cross stitch.

Right: *Duke*, 2018,
45 x 55cm
(18 x 21½in).
Mixed media.

Lace

Lace has always been valued for its craftsmanship and sophistication and has been used for many centuries to embellish clothes and household items. We mainly think of it now as an edging trim, but beautiful collars, garments and shawls have been made from lace and it is still a staple of wedding-dress design in the 21st century. Making lace by hand was a thriving industry in Europe from the 17th century, the two main types being bobbin lace and needle lace. It was used to signify status and power by both men and women. In the 20th century, the production of lace was transformed by mechanization and in the UK Nottingham became renowned for its machine-made lace which made lace cheaper and available to all. Handmade lace continued to be made by hobbyists and for couture but became rarer, though it is still made today.

There are many different ways to produce handmade lace and, despite there being many identification books, it is sometimes difficult for the novice to date and work out the provenance of lace that you might be given or pick up in an antique market. I can just about identify handmade bobbin lace, which is made by winding threads round bobbins which are then wrapped round pins on a pillow, and Venetian needle lace which is made using a needle

and thread and from hundreds of small stitches. When purchasing lace or using donations I look for delicate, fragile, even yellowing pieces rather than heavy crocheted doilies. It is unlikely you will find good examples of lace other than in antique shops or fairs though black lace dresses can be found second hand and black lace never seems to look as 'cheap' as its white nylon equivalent. If you are lucky enough to find lace collars, they can be used in the traditional way to add to the sophistication of a garment. Really special pieces of fine lace I like to remount on to a dark colour and frame so they are presented on the wall as the works of art I consider them to be. I attach the lace as invisibly as possible to the background fabric and, when mounting, make sure the board is acid free. My mother collected lace and was particularly proud of a piece of Leavers lace from the 1890s. It was probably from Calais and made by machine to emulate Mechlin bobbin lace. The Victoria and Albert Museum have a sample of this same lace. Below, I have attached my mother's fragment to a blue background, inspired by a Nottingham lace commercial traveller's sample book where all the examples are attached to blue paper. I have created a little collage around it using bits of my quilts which bring her and my textile stories together.

Left: *Leavers Lace*, 2019, 22 x 13.5cm (8½ x 5½in). 19th century French lace used within textile collage.

Above: Donya Coward, *Magpie*, 2015. Mixed media.

Donya Coward

Donya Coward is an artist based in Nottingham, a city in England famous for its development of machine lace. The artist utilizes both vintage hand and machine lace in the development of many of her sculptural pieces which have been called 'textile taxidermy'. Like the magpies she portrays, Donya is a bit of a magpie herself as she recycles and collects haberdashery, old clothes, lace and costume jewellery. Her eclectic collection of materials is key to informing the nature of the beast or bird she is portraying. Any marks, stains or wear and tear in the fabrics is incorporated and adds character. Donya starts with an armature that is adapted and sculpted and on to which she stitches and blends small exquisite pieces that are worked separately to capture the textures and plumage of the bird. These elements, for example a wing or breast or head, can be hand or machine stitched and are layered with lace, and further tiny fragments of fabric or thread or found objects are appliquéd on to the surface. Beading and sequins are sometimes used to add lustre and echo the sheen of the plumage.

Right: Donya Coward, *Pigeon*, 2017. Mixed media.

Lace Sketchbook

Lace has inspired many artists over the centuries, who have delighted in painting its intricacies. I, too, have found it is something to turn to in sketchbook development where I can easily incorporate it into mixed-media ideas which are sometimes taken into printmaking, particularly monotypes.

I love trying to capture the patterns within the lace by drawing with pencil, pen and ink or sewing machine. I will often work from behind the page using a photocopy of the lace itself to guide me. Sometimes I incorporate an actual piece of lace into the drawing.

Ayrshine Work 1840

Lace Books

Above: I was
fortunate to find
some lace-making
patterns printed
on to fabric which
I have sewn
together and used
as the cover of my
lace book.

Left: Lace
sketchbook.
Drawing and mixed
media inspired by
and using old lace.

In this section I encourage you to have a go at making two types of lace book that can show off your best examples of lace.

In past times, manufacturers of lace put their samples into books or ledgers for salesmen to show to potential trade customers. The little snippets would be glued to the pages, which were sometimes coloured paper, to show the lace to its best advantage. You can do the same thing with your own lace, displaying it in book form where the pages can be turned and shared with others. I do not like the way glue can potentially discolour or damage textiles so I sew my fragments on to pages made from an old wool blanket with collaged fabrics underneath the lace, as shown overleaf.

To do it yourself:

1 Cut three double-page spreads of either a piece of old blanket or another suitable fabric. I have chosen blanket because it is easy to sink your stitches into and work it so the stitches do not show on the other side. My double-page spread size was 34 x 18cm (13½ x 7in) but you could make them any size. Once you have folded these pieces in the middle this will give you six leaves and therefore twelve pages.

2 Gather your pieces of lace and a selection of other fabrics – I have decided to use just white or cream lace. Have a go at laying bits of lace over the top of the fabric scraps to see what they look like. I think lace looks great over greys, dark browns, blacks and neutrals, so that forms my own palette of background fabrics. You could, however, choose another colour story, for example, a range of blues combined with the lace on a pale blue blanket.

3 Start to layer small pieces of fabric on one side of the double-page spread and then choose one of your pieces of lace to place on top. You are almost certainly going to have to cut or tear it smaller. Sometimes I layer the lace too, particularly if it has an awkward edge shape. Pin together and move on to the other half of the blanket page.

4 Continue to build up all twelve collages, remembering you are using both sides of the blanket to achieve this. Every now and then fold the blanket in half and interleaf the pages to get a feel of how the collages interact with each other.

5 Stitch all your pieces on using a tiny stab stitch and if possible just sinking into the middle of the blanket with your needle rather than going through to the other side and spoiling the collage on the reverse. Once I have done this I often add further decorative stitches, using a crochet cotton that matches the colour of the lace.

6 Choose something for the cover and cut it slightly larger than the blanket pages – about 1.5cm (½in) bigger all the way round. I have sourced some old lace-making patterns for my cover but I have also used pieces of quilt, linen and furnishing fabrics for the covers of other books. Decide on the order of your pages and then bulldog clip the book together flat. You might like to mark the middle fold in some way. Sew together with stitches up the middle or use pamphlet stitch as I have done. (Details for working this simple stitch are readily available online.)

Above: *Lace Book*, 2017. Lace and fabric attached to wool-blanket pages with additional embroidery.

If you cannot face such a big project as making a fabric lace book like the one on pages 90–91, then you might like to use a ready-made book to showcase snippets of lace. I have chosen to use very old books with black endpapers. These were not expensive and were easy to find as a century ago, nearly every family owned a hymnal and prayer book so they regularly turn up in flea markets and second-hand bookshops. You are going to make a collage so you need to remove all the pages to keep just the flat book covers to mount your work on. I do not cut the pages out but tear these away from the spine, a small section at a time, as I love the exposed rough spine visible at the end. Keep any pages that are significant, such as those with a name and date or which are black as you may be able to use them. Now gather your materials, including lace. You are going to use tiny amounts but it is good to have a choice.

In my collages I have incorporated:

- Old documents and letters.

- Crepe paper which has had a wash of watercolour.

- Brown wrapping paper which has been lightly brushed with household emulsion paint.

- Pieces of wallpaper.

- Fabrics, particularly with frayed edges or interesting textures.

- Sheer fabric.

- Handmade paper and other found papers.

Start to cut or tear small pieces from your collage kit and lay them out on top of the open book boards. Remember that the objective is to make a piece of lace the focus of the composition. Choose a small section of perhaps torn lace to complement the other elements. You will need to decide whether you are going to make separate collages on each book end or work across the spine. I love the raggedy spine, so tend to leave this as visible as possible. Now comes the hard bit as you will have lots of tiny fragile elements that are easily displaced. I now use pins or tiny amounts of a dry glue stick to partly stick the whole thing together. Once this is dry, I sew the fabric elements on to the paper elements and decorate with a few stitches. When you are happy with the collage, stick it into the book cover and then it can be framed or propped up.

French Finds

If you have ever been to a French brocante or vide grenier you will know these are the most amazing places to find beautiful antique French linens and lace. There are websites now dedicated to listing when and where they are on and, if you can't get to France yourself, you should be able to source French antiques and linen from your armchair as there are many dealers selling items through Instagram, Etsy and Ebay. The main thing to look for is authentic French linen or flax goods which are of the highest quality. Artisanal smocks, chemises, nightdresses, sheets, tableclothes, napkins and hand towels can usually be found in most markets. These may well have been part of a trousseau, made as a dowry for a bride by mothers and grandmothers. Much of this antique linen will be from the late 19th century. The general advice would be to seek out pieces that are not stained, darned or poorly sewn, but these are, in fact, my favourite pieces. You need to get to a market early as there are many traders who buy the best to take back and sell at a profit in the UK. You will pay less if you buy from a trader who has not ironed, starched and 'styled' the products and certainly less than from an antique shop. I also look for thick French quilts, called boutis, which often have a quilted top and bottom fabric which you can strip away and use. There are, of course, printed fabrics too including the famous French toile de Jouy fabrics. I look for old curtains and pieces of upholstery you can cut up. If I can get to a market, I always look for more unusual things such as old sacks, children's clothes, trimmings and fabric bags. Sometimes these are so beautiful or interesting that I do not 'use' them but hang them up as pieces of art.

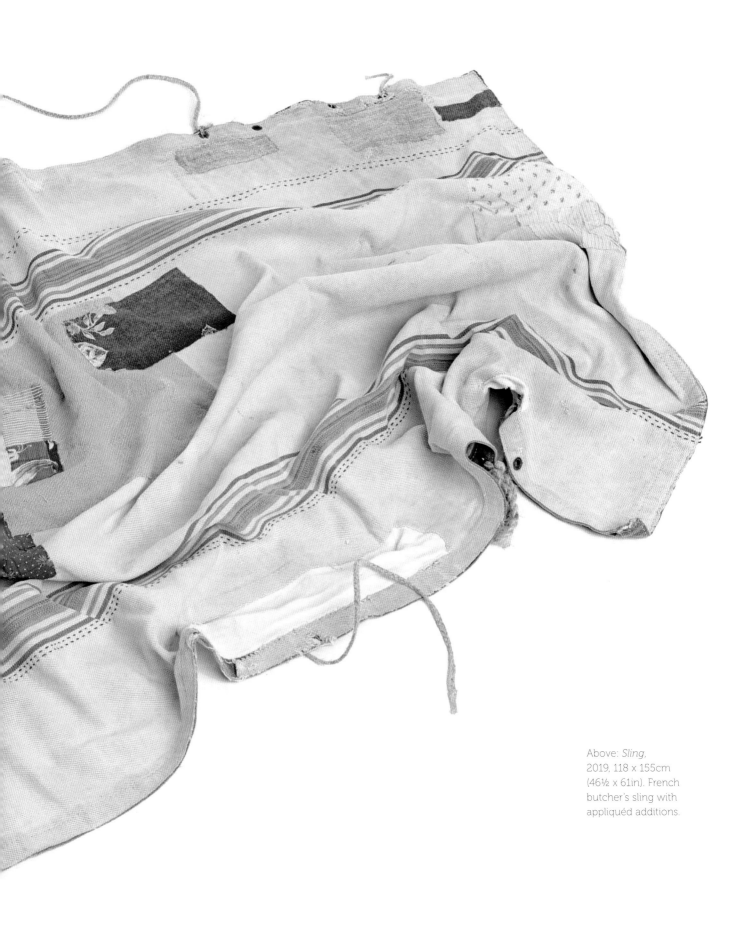

Above: *Sling*,
2019, 118 x 155cm
(46½ x 61in). French
butcher's sling with
appliquéd additions.

Above: Two French linen napkins with monograms and floral addition.

Napkins and Towels

Antique French linen napkins are a joy to own and when I open them up I like to think that they were used at many convivial meal times and then lovingly laundered, folded and starched before the next meal. I have a set that are only used at Christmas and they add a sense of luxury, particularly when matched with a white linen tablecloth. If they are from the 19th or early 20th century most will have a hand-embroidered set of initials or an interlinked monogram in the corner. This was to identify them in laundering, as household linen was often washed at communal washhouses, *lavoires*, near rivers, by household staff. Often, as in my examples, a red thread was used, probably madder dyed as this would not run. Monograms were embroidered on to sheets and hand towels too and it was a skill learnt by young girls so they could prepare the vast amount of linen needed for their trousseaux. Inevitably the ones you find will not be your own initials, but you could 'tag' them as I have here with little scraps of French fabrics.

Napkins and hand towels are so easy to find that I have no qualms in cutting them up and have often made them into cushions. I sometimes use them as pages for my fabric books and frequently use them to wrap things up in. They are very easy to over-dye. In *French Book* I have cut up an old hand towel into pages and then created little collages from pieces of quilt in the centre of each page, leaving plenty of white space round the collage to really draw the eye in. The towel was thin with wear, so I backed each page with calico. I have used a piece of worn coverlet for the cover and have sewn the whole thing together by wrapping another piece of linen round the spine and securing it with buttons.

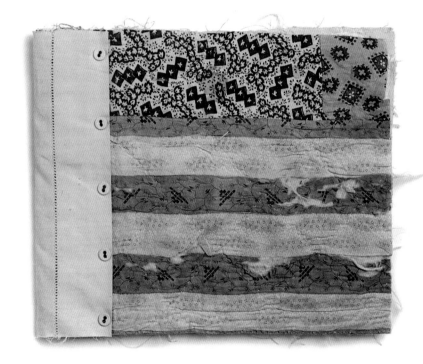

Top: *French Book*, 2017. Each page is 30 x 24cm (12 x 9½in) Linen teacloths were cut into the pages for this book which holds little collages and touches of stitching.

Above: An old piece of quilt has been used for the cover of *French Book* and a pillowcase edge used for the spine. Buttons secure the cover and pages.

Right: 19th century linen smock appliquéd with flowers unpicked from a French boutis.

French Smocks

I have been lucky enough to be asked to teach in France several times and particularly love the opportunity to shop in local markets. When I am teaching at the beautiful Chateau Dumas near Toulouse, an added highlight of the week, for both the students and me, is the visit from a local dealer who brings her wares to us, laying them out under the trees for us to look at and buy. I have purchased several linen smocks and chore shirts, probably dating from the late 19th and early 20th centuries which I believe are hand woven from locally grown flax. Most have a V-section pieced into the side seams because the fabric was quite narrow – the maximum width of the loom. They are nearly all monogrammed and hand sewn with tiny stitches and French seams. The fabric has incredible strength and will even put up with being boiled, though some smocks do show signs of darning and mending. I overdyed the one illustrated here and then embellished it on the hem and sleeves with appliquéd flowers unpicked from a French boutis quilt.

Ticking

Ticking is a tightly woven fabric that was used for many centuries as a mattress fabric because straw, or the quills of feathers, were unable to poke through the weave, ensuring a better night's sleep. The woven stripes are usually black or blue and can come in various widths. I know when I have sourced an authentic vintage mattress ticking as there is evidence of feathers or down stuck to the back of the fabric. It is now reproduced – sometimes the stripes are printed instead of woven – and it has become a beloved staple of designers and has moved out of the bedroom to being used for curtains, pillows, bags and garments. It seems it never goes out of fashion.

I have recently started using ticking and other vintage fabrics to make bags for ongoing sewing projects in my studio. I am trying to cut down on the use of plastic in my workspace – it has been too easy to get organised by throwing things into plastic bags without thinking of the environmental impact. I have, in fact, found it a delight to make bags and smaller purses for my own use and to keep things gathered for teaching. They are certainly more aesthetically pleasing, although it is sometimes a challenge to keep the stripes straight! In the bag shown below I have made use of patching that was already there and I have had to do some additional patching myself in order to get enough fabric to make a small project bag. I had to mend a little tear too. On the inside of the bag I have used hook-and-loop tape as I did not want any fastening to detract from the design of the front. The buttons are merely decorative. If you are using ticking, then consider mixing it with a plain colour or denim, combining different sorts of ticking stripes and being more inventive with it. The great French artist, Louise Bourgeois, made artwork with ticking, using traditional patchwork techniques but creating, in some instances, an almost Op Art illusion through the effective use of the stripes.

Right: Ticking bag, 2019. French mattress ticking and linen-covered buttons. The patchwork star shows how you can use the stripes to good effect.

Toile de Jouy

Toile de Jouy became popular in France in the 18th century. The original manufacturing of this classic French printed fabric started in Jouy-en-Josas, a village near Versailles. It falls into two styles of design, floral and narrative. The floral toiles were mostly block printed, multi coloured and sometimes drew their inspiration from Indian chintz design. They were ideal for both dress and interior furnishings. The narrative prints were usually monochrome and featured complex vignettes drawn from a vision of an idealised pastoral life but also scenes from history, opera and mythology.

Toile de Jouy has never gone out of fashion and is still being reproduced or being reimagined by contemporary designers such as Timorous Beasties, who twist and subvert the narratives, bringing them up to date. You can find fine printed French fabrics at antique fairs but if you are in France look in antique shops there. Some of my toiles have been unpicked from the top of French boutis quilts. More locally, you may be lucky enough to persuade an interior design shop to give you old sample books but also look on Ebay where it is easy to find these iconic fabrics for sale.

In some instances the unpicked toile surface maybe very fragile and you may need to iron on fusible web to give it strength, as I have done on the waistcoat shown opposite.

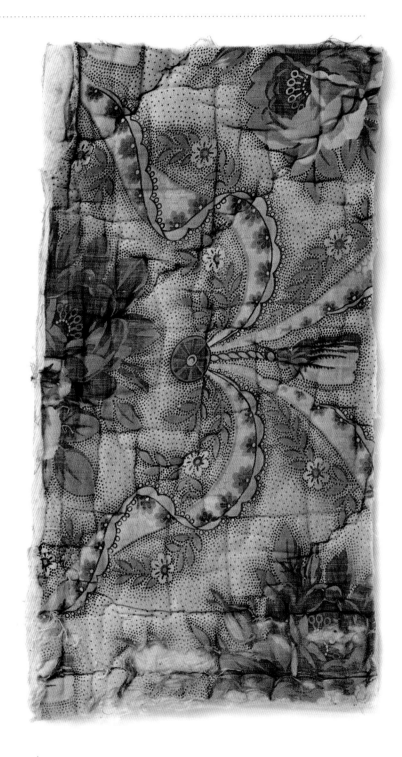

Above and right: A piece of boutis quilt, featuring a French printed design, has been deconstructed and applied to a child's waistcoat.

Above: *Matin*, 2019, 48 x 52cm (19 x 20½in). A fragment of toile de Jouy used as the centre of a patchwork of dressmaking scraps and vintage materials.

I tend to use my toile de Jouy pieces as the focal point for a collage as I have done above in *Matin*. It is surrounded by dressmaking fabric scraps and an extra layer of surface embellishment has been added with hundreds of seed stitches which echo the engraving marks. You could stitch into the scene itself with colour or subvert the narrative by extracting and replacing or defacing the idyll.

Grain Sacks

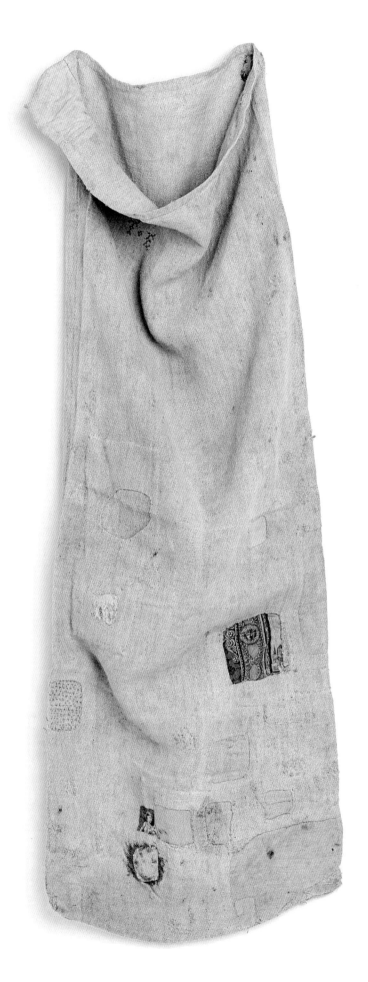

In France it is easy to come by hessian and cotton sack bags which were used to store grain or walnuts. These would be heavily used and reused, and thrifty farmers and their wives would keep them together by darning and patching. Sometimes the patching would be on the surface like appliqué and at other times from behind. It is not always hand stitched – in some sacks there is evidence that glue was involved. These are probably my favourite French finds as they have such a history shown through this unselfconscious mending. I rarely intervene with this precious landscape of marks but here I have made my mark a little by inserting a luxury toile de Jouy into the mix.

Left and below (detail): Very old French patched and darned grain sack with appliquéd toile de Jouy.

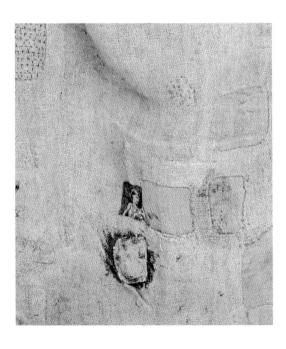

CHAPTER FOUR

Wardrobe

In this final chapter I take a quick look in the closet. We live in an era in which clothes are now so cheap that they have almost become single-use items and the methods of production for many garments have a negative impact on the environment and rely on cheap labour. We all have too many clothes and accessories and even donating to a charity shop doesn't mean that your cast-offs will not end up in landfill. Much better to transform your own or vintage items into something really special and, even if you don't use or wear them again, they will become something you might want to hang up on the wall or display rather than throw away.

Left: Detail of
Maenson, a wall
hanging made from
deconstructing
men's suits (see
also page 109).

The Little Dress

I love dresses and often personalize my own clothing with a tiny fabric addition that makes something high street a little bit more unique and personal. A tiny bit of Liberty fabric added to a cuff or placket, a little patchwork or a bit of embroidery makes me feel my garments are special. For the purpose of this book, though, I am talking about transforming something vintage or second hand, rather than from the high street, and adding to its story. I like to source old things, but sometimes something more recent will do if it has a lived-in and loved look about it. *Blue Dress* was found in a charity shop and was pretty worn out but the label in the neckline showed it was just from a high street shop. I have used the grid of the weave to work a bit of cross stitch into the piece and made hexagons which have been appliquéd rather than patched together in the usual way. I like to hang my pieces up to display but this does not mean that I have not sewn them with care so they could be used for a special occasion even if they would not withstand repeated washing.

Here is what you could do with an old dress, whether it be a child's or doll's dress or an adult item:

- Change the buttons.

- Add fabric to the hem.

- Hand stitch some additional decorative elements.

- Appliqué elements from a patterned fabric.

- Add a pocket or reinforce the pocket with a binding of fabric along the top.

- Patch fabrics on to the dress whether it needs mending or not.

- Use haberdashery such as rickrack or ribbons.

- Over-dye the fabric.

Below: *Blue Dress*, 2016. Charity-shop find that has been embellished with patchwork and cross stitch.

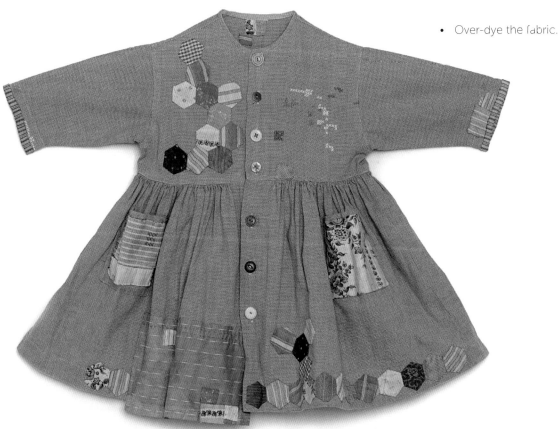

Right: Baby gown, 2019. Patchwork and appliqué.

Above: Baby gown, 2019. Wool and ribbon embroidery.

The Baby Dress

Christening robes have traditionally been white but times have moved on and what I have made here could be worn with a bright little T-shirt underneath for a contemporary Christening or naming ceremony. You need to take special care with making something for a baby, even if it is to be worn for just a few hours. Wash the garment with a gentle non-biological soap and also wash any other materials you are going to appliqué on to the surface. Ensure that there are no ligature risks with ties or choking hazards with buttons. With these very old baby gowns I have turned them inside out to expose the quilted bodice that was often hidden inside the garment. One garment has been embroidered with wool to complement the wool flannel of the foundation garment and the other has been patchworked. In the appliqué process edges have been turned under, as this dress will probably need laundering after wearing and fraying is not an option.

Suit Yourself

In my book *Textile Collage* (Batsford, 2016) I showed how
you can customize jackets with broderie perse stitch, and
appliqué, but here I want to explore how you can transform
a man's jacket into something else through deconstruction.
The deconstruction process will allow you to accumulate
a range of flatter fabrics and textures. It is hard to take
scissors to a piece of wearable clothing, but careful cutting
away will reveal the inner workings of the tailoring and
construction. Padding elements, tacking stitches, reinforcing
and inner seams will all become evident through careful
unpicking and removal of the lining fabric. I approach this
deconstruction process methodically. I cut away the pocket
areas and front lapels first and keep the back of the collar
and manufacturer's labels. I then cut off the sleeves just
above the sleeve insertion and down through the seam
of the sleeve. It is in these top shoulder pads that you will
find layers of fabric and complicated overlays. These might
be small pieces but are all kept. The backs of jackets are
less interesting but, if cut away carefully, may give you a
larger piece of good-quality wool or tweed to use in other
ways. You can now mix the fabrics into other projects or
challenge yourself by trying to create something just from
that one jacket.

In *Maenson* I combined the most interesting pieces from a
few jackets to create a wall piece. I have attached them to
a piece of felt with discreet hand stitching. The edges are
uneven because I have used the curves, lapels and other
features of the jacket at the edge. The piece went through
many changes at the laying-out stage; it is not easy to do
this freeform style of patchwork, particularly when there
are curved edges on some pieces. When I had finished,
I thought it a little dull so have inserted some tiny patches
of Liberty fabric, mixing in a little femininity perhaps to the
masculine jacket fragments.

Right: *Maenson*,
2018. 55 x 95cm
(21½ x 37½in).
Men's suit jackets
have been
deconstructed
and patchworked
together to form a
new piece of cloth.

Book Jacket

Left: *Random Musings and Observations of Happenings*, 2019. The pages of this book made from my dad's best suit have been held together through a piece of fabric wrapped round the spine and secured by the Polo mints found in his pocket.

Left: *Random Musings and Observations of Happenings*, 2019. Transferred photograph of my dad, collage of pieces taken from his jacket and text taken from his memoirs.

My dad died in a care home, and at the end of his life he cared little about clothes so most of what he left was literally threadbare. He did not want us to buy him new things and said his limited worn wardrobe would 'see him out'. The only piece of clothing that was worth keeping was his best suit and this was probably because he rarely wore it. I hung the suit in my own wardrobe, and seeing it would remind me of him, but eventually I had to make my own mark on it. A fabric book seemed appropriate as the 'pages' could be photographed and then reproduced to share with the rest of the family. I made a template of the page size and tried to cut the suit into this format but found that sometimes I had to patch pieces together to make the internal workings of the suit more evident. My father's letters and the memories he wrote in later life were much treasured, so, although I have included photographs (which were transferred on to fabric), the words were the most important part of the story. I did not want to reveal all, as they are a private family memory, but I have chosen phrases and hand embroidered them on to cloth that had been close to his body. To do this yourself, enlarge the words to the size you want and then use dressmaker's carbon underneath and draw through on to the cloth. You will have to press very hard and use 'fresh' carbon paper (I used white) as this is not totally effective on wool cloth. When embroidering, you must also refer to the original script to capture the individuality of the handwriting. After a while I found that I did not use the carbon paper as I got into a rhythm and with careful observation was able to stitch the handwriting without a guide. I have worked mostly in couching using a perle thread.

I have used a jacket, but you could use other items of clothing with personal resonance, creating something that holds memories and stories for you. A patchwork is the most obvious thing to make and quilts have always contained pieces of family fabrics, but it might be enough for you just to take a snippet of a loved one's garment and sew it into the inside of one of your own pieces of clothing to make that link.

The Shirt

The shirt has been with us for many hundreds of years and has gone through many incarnations to suit the costume style and working needs of each generation. Originally it was worn exclusively by men, but in the 19th century women started to wear shirts too and have done ever since. I recycle all of my own and my husband's shirts for projects. They have been washed frequently so are very soft and particularly useful for appliqué. I cut off the collar, the cuffs, pockets and opening buttonholes and buttons. All get used eventually. Artist Ali Ferguson takes the deconstruction one step further than I do, re-piecing individual sections and creating a story.

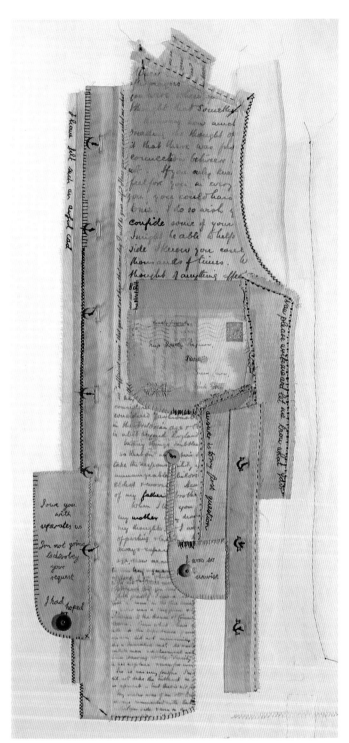

Above: Ali Ferguson, (Hi)Stories Uncovered – *Gillie's Shirt*, 2016. Pre-owned shirt coloured with gesso, walnut ink and tea staining, inkjet-printed fabrics and abaca paper, silk organza and hand stitching.

Ali Ferguson

Much of Ali Ferguson's textile practice revolves around the thought that fabric captures and holds 'memory' – that an old piece of clothing is implanted with stories of the wearer, or a piece of stitched table linen holds within it the secrets of a household.

Gillie's Shirt is part of her (Hi)Stories Uncovered series in which, inspired by forensic examination and the collection of evidence, she has quite literally taken apart a garment piece by piece to reveal imagined emotional traces left behind by someone who has touched the wearer in some way. Her evidence came from Gillie's handwritten letters in the 1920s, declaring his love to a Miss Dorothy Ferguson. Clearly she had made a significant impression on him. Ali uses an inkjet printer to copy paragraphs from the letters on to fabric and abaca paper, and excerpts of these are highlighted with hand stitching. The letters and shirt are not actually connected apart from in Ali's imagination. However, the shirt does bring its own hidden stories to the piece as does the beautiful old silk organza tablecloth used as her background fabric. Ali loves the idea of these stories interweaving with each other.

Collars

Detachable collars first became available in the 1830s and were sometimes sold separately from the shirt itself. It is believed they were invented by an American called Hannah Montague who was fed up with washing her blacksmith husband's shirts when only the collars were dirty and so started to cut them off, launder them separately and sew them on again. A manufacturing plant for the collars grew up in her hometown of Troy. The shirt collar and cuffs were the most visible part of the shirt and would attract more dirt so making the collar detachable meant that it could not only be laundered separately but also starched at a time when the fashion was for extremely stiff collars. Cuffs and sometimes even fronts could be detached from shirts too. The vogue for stiff detachable collars lasted until the 1930s and they are still used by some professions – the law, the clergy and the military. Starching went out of fashion and it became easier to launder a whole shirt.

I now like to work with soft collars which are not white, mostly sourced from France, and I will use them almost as a notebook to capture phrases that are important to me. The set shown below has Make Do and Mend quotes embroidered into the back of each collar, which is the part most likely to be worn through rubbing against the neck. Sometimes it is just a pleasure to transform the collar through appliqué and stitch.

Above: A worn collar has been the base for a little textile collage enhanced with St George's cross stitch.

Below: Make Do and Mend messages have been embroidered into the back of these stiff collars in the place where they are most likely to wear and be mended.

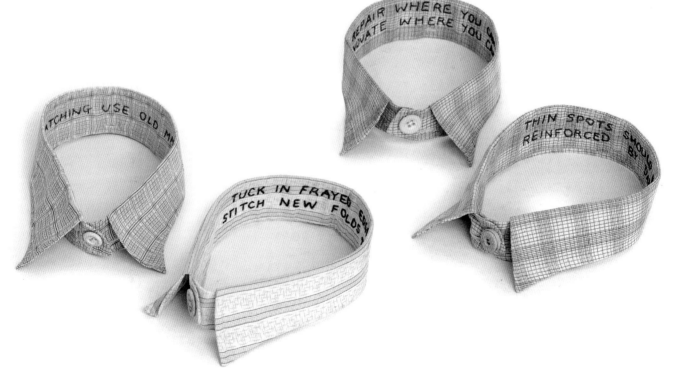

Right: *A Pocket Full of Flowers*, 2016. A pocket acts as a vase in this composition, worked on an old piece of quilt.

Pockets

Pockets are designed to be useful and can be embellished while in their original position on the front of a shirt or a jacket, or on the back of a pair of jeans, or they can be removed and reused. Fashion designers have often drawn attention to a pocket by using a trim and you can do the same with fabric, trim or stitch embellishment. You could acknowledge their original purpose by sewing lots of pockets on to a firm base and then hanging it up to provide a storage solution, or even just sewing one on to the outside or inside of a home-made bag. If you collect enough you could create a pocket book, using the pockets to store, for example, letters or documents. If I am recycling garments I always cut off the pockets with the idea that I will maybe sew them on to another garment or project one day, but in my own practice the most use I have found for them is to provide a quirky vase shape for my vases of flowers collages.

War Widows' Stories Quilt 2018–2020

arthur+martha is an experimental arts organization whose aim is to bring attention to the visions and words of people who are sometimes lost in the corners, such as the homeless and older people. Through writing and art workshops they help build confidence and raise self-esteem. The War Widows' Stories project shares the voices of war's forgotten women, left behind after the loss of their loved ones in the service of their country. This project allowed war widows to create a block for a quilt, building a creative legacy and a shared history. The quilt itself touches on universal themes of bereavement, sacrifice, courage and love. Many of the women used pieces of shirting or pockets as the canvas for their thoughts. One participant, Lauran Hamilton, writes of her pocket:

Below: Lauran Hamilton, *Lauran's Pocket*, 2018. A deeply moving embroidered pocket, one of the blocks contributing to the War Widows' Stories Quilt 2018–2020.

'The red cross is for four dead soldiers. The green at the top of the pocket represents the gorse bushes that grew in the area where they died. The silver thread is the grey of the twisted Land Rover. The green is the grass in the field. The brown is the turned-over soil of the land, mixed with the blood of the four men. The yellow and purple are the flowers from the hedgerows. Sewing my square gave me a strange sort of peace. I could think about how [my husband] died while I stitched, so the sewing was giving me control. It's hard to explain, but it worked for me.'

The Headscarf

I love many of the designs that you see on old scarves, particularly the upmarket head scarves of the type that the Queen wears so stylishly (often by Hermes), but in reality it is rare to find these pure silk scarves cheaply. A few years ago, I wanted to see if I could work with those unloved and ugly scarves made of polyester, acrylic, rayon and viscose that you see in dump bins in almost every charity shop. The scarves were too thin to embroider on to or easily patchwork together so manipulating them seemed the answer. I was inspired by an old yoyo quilt I had in which Suffolk puffs had been made from silky rayons and other man-made fabrics and then attached to an eiderdown. I started to make Suffolk puffs from the scarves with the intention of attaching them to a foundation in the same way they had been attached to the eiderdown. The reuse of the scarves coincided with decorating a room and sourcing old furniture to do up, and so they were eventually used to transform a comfortable, but ugly, easy chair and there were enough left over to use on a lampshade as well.

Left: Suffolk puffs chair, 2007. Chair reupholstered with patchwork and Suffolk puffs made from headscarves.

Below: Lampshade, 2007. Recovered with a patchwork of head scarves and appliquéd suffolk puffs.

I am not an upholsterer so a certain amount of problem solving had to take place, and I ironed a stabilizer fabric on to flat scarves and then patchworked these together to make a surface with which I could upholster the chair and on to which I could apply the Suffolk puffs. I actually hand sewed the patchwork base with the puffs attached to the ugly velvet upholstery of the chair. The same was done for the lampshade. These are pieces that I sometimes love for their uniqueness and unconventional use of difficult fabrics and at other times I feel they are just over the top and a bit kitsch. The point is that sometimes you have to work outside your comfort zone (mine is timeworn fabrics) and take risks in order to come up with new concepts.

Manipulation

Scarves tend to be made of a thin fabric with a nice drape and this can be put to good effect with fabric manipulation, such as the Suffolk puffs, or, as I have found through experimentation, pleating. I am fortunate enough to own a Princess Pleater which makes this job very easy. This little machine has a set of curved needles that act in conjunction with the grooves of a number of rollers. You feed the fabric in at the back and it goes through the rollers and out on to the threaded needles and creates a pleated fabric. It was designed to make smocking easier, but you can create samples that can be used within corsage making, as an insert in a garment, or as a piece in itself if you stitch into it. You can put paper through it and you can layer up fabrics if they are very lightweight. I like the way it distorts images, as in this horse-racing scarf which is made of man-made fabric. You can make the pleats more permanent by steaming. I bundle the pleated fabric, with all the threads tied off at the side, into a piece of aluminium foil and then put it into the basket of my vegetable steamer and steam for about half an hour. You are then able to pull out the threads if you wish.

Below: A horse-racing themed scarf has been pushed through a Princess Pleater. It provides a permanently manipulated piece of fabric that could be used in many projects.

Ties

There are many wonderful tutorials on the internet showing you how to transform ties into bags, belts, skirts and cushions, but I wanted to do something a bit more personal with my dad's and my husband's old ties and have integrated them into a chair which is in constant use in our dining room. You need a chair with a loose bottom that can be removed. I then created a patchwork using the widest part of the ties and machine stitched them together with a zig-zag stitch from the back. The patchwork was organized to be big enough to stretch over the seat and then was stapled underneath and the seat pad replaced. The back of the chair was made entirely of wood but nevertheless I made a second patchwork of the remaining parts of the ties, handstitched on the labels and turned the seams to the exact size of a template of that area of the chair. I sewed these seams down at the back and then glued the fabric addition into place using a glue gun.

Left: Tie chair, 2010. The seat and back of this chair have been reupholstered with a patchwork of family ties.

Buckles and Belts

You may have a belt from a dress that is no longer worn in your wardrobe, have taken a belt off a vintage garment or found one in a charity shop. If they are made of cloth rather than leather they can be transformed through a variety of textile techniques. Here are three examples, and if you don't end up wearing your beautifully crafted belt you can always just hang it up. The white belt, which I was told came from a tennis dress, has been made more special through a scattering of mother of pearl and French glass buttons. The pale blue belt has given me a chance to use the tiniest scraps of Liberty fabric and I have used finger turned appliqué to ensure the belt is serviceable. The top belt has been constructed from scratch on a piece of robust cloth, and favourite elements, including a piece of cross stitch worked by my mother, have been further embellished with my own cross stitch scattered across them. In each case I have added a buckle and you might need to do this if there is just a loop or popper fastening. The buckle can be placed in such a way that it is functional or decorative with poppers still in place underneath to hold the belt together.

Buckles can be used in other ways, for example as a special feature at the top of a piece of textile jewellery, but you will need to glue a brooch fastening of an appropriate size on to the back of the buckle in order to be able to pin it on a garment. I also attach buckles, which I have usually found nestling in old button tins, to grosgrain ribbon and use them to strap up my fabric bundles. It keeps the fabrics snug and neat and is aesthetically pleasing.

Above: These three belts have been decorated with textile collage and stitch (top), finger turned appliqué using Liberty-print fabrics (centre) and glass and mother of pearl buttons to echo a beautiful buckle (bottom).

Worn By

I would like to finish the book with a personal project that became the subject for an exhibition, and for which I spent a little more time deconstructing and combining three or four garments into new and resolved two-dimensional compositions.

Over the years, I have sourced historical garments, particularly from the late Victorian and Edwardian periods, from vintage textile fairs. Many of these have had a spell hanging from the back of the door in my studio and this chance to live with them has gradually revealed their stories and secrets. I have never paid very much for the pieces so the garments are often very worn, patched and any silk elements shredded. They are in an unwearable state. To protect them a little, at some point I turned them inside out and found that, actually, I was more interested in them this way. The inner workings and construction, evidence of tacking stitches, mending and neat French seams exposed the hand of the maker more fully than the 'best' side. Some of the garments still carried staining from sweat and skin, and handling parts of clothing which have been in touch with another woman's body created an emotional link between me and the anonymous wearer. It was a big thing for me to take a pair of scissors to these beautiful and possibly valuable clothes but that is what I did. I wanted to create new 'landscape' pieces which mixed up and turned the functional garments into delicate abstract assemblages on which I could make my own traces through drawing with thread.

I cut away the more interesting parts first, sometimes cutting an obvious shape, for example an armhole, pocket detail, buttonholes, suggestions of bodice or neckline. Sometimes I unpicked to open up the seams and I also unpicked the lace and other decorative elements from blouse fronts. These were handled, turned over, examined, mixed up in a disorderly fashion (always a good way for me of getting going) before I started to pull together the compositions and lay them on to a wadding. I made a set of twenty collages and worked on the composition of all of them at once so I could judge their relationship to each other. My aim was to draw the attention of the viewer to the seams, edges and construction as well as mixing up the materials. It was only when I had attached the fabrics to the backing that I could start to consider the marks I made myself. These are sometimes linear stitches which lead the eye across the piece to an interesting detail or which emphasise an edge, or they are scatter stitches that help to blend individual elements.

Left: *Worn*, 2016. Edwardian and Victorian garments have been deconstructed to provide the ingredients for these collages which draw the viewer's attention to the small details of garment construction.

Right: Mood board made in an old print tray.

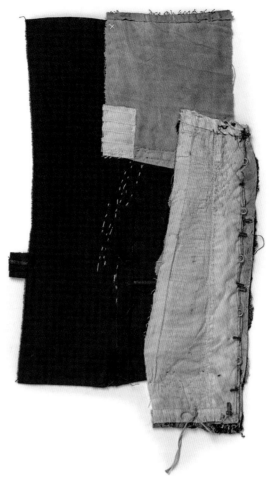

Left: 'Worn', 2016. Three of the twenty collages I made emphasising the construction of old garments.

For all of my projects there are often tiny scraps left over and even these were used within a book structure, as a tiny mood board and to create a linear narrative that could be wound on to a cotton reel and be exposed or tightly wrapped up.

You may not have access to such old pieces, though it is easier now to source them online, but you could try taking several worn garments, as I did, cut them up and see where it takes you. I chose the garments carefully so that the palette of colours was pleasing and in the compositions I could work with tonal contrasts. You could try putting one black garment into the mix which might have the same effect.

Conclusion

I hope that you have been inspired by my examples and projects, and will start to think about using old textiles that you have accumulated or inherited and turn them into something else, or make your own personal mark on them. By using second hand and what you already have, you are committing to a green agenda and you are adding value through your personal creative input. If you can use cloth that has a family connection, then the handling and stitching will have even deeper meaning. In the end, it isn't even about the finished product but about enjoying the process of making it.

Below: Fragile deconstructed quilt cloth is wrapped for safekeeping round an old weaving bobbin.

Artists

Ali Ferguson: aliferguson.co.uk

Alice Pattullo: alicepattullo.com

Ann Stephens: annstephens.co.uk

arthur+martha: arthur-martha.com

Colin Millington: paffronandscott.co.uk

Donya Coward: donyacoward.co.uk

Ellie Langley: ellielangley.com

Hannah Lamb: hannahlamb.co.uk

Liz Jones: Instagram @lizjonesmakes

Mandy James: Instagram @littleragbooks

Mandy Pattullo: mandypattullo.co.uk

Ruth Singer: ruthsinger.com

Ulla-Stina Wikander: ullastinawikander.com

Further Reading

Celant, Germano, Louise Bourgeois, *The Fabric Works*, Skira, 2010.

Court, Sibella, *Etcetera*, Murdoch Books, 2009.

Court, Sibella, *Bowerbird*, ABC Books, 2012.

Edwards, Joan, *Crewel Embroidery in England*, Batsford, 1975.

Falick, Melanie, *Making a Life*, Artisan Books, 2019.

Kettle, Alice and McKeating, Jane, *Hand Stitch: Perspectives*, Bloomsbury, 2012.

Lamb, Hannah, *Poetic Cloth*, Batsford, 2019.

Howard, Constance, *The Constance Howard Book of Stitches*, Batsford, 1979.

Hill, June and Dr. Jennifer Harris (Eds), *Primmy Chorley: Another World*, Ruthin Craft Centre, 2019.

Kabur, Anu, Pink, Anu and Meriste, Mai, *Designs and Patterns from Muhu Island*, Saara Publishing House, 2011.

Kyoichi, Tsuziki, *Boro: Rags and Tatters from the far North of Japan*, Aspect Corp, 2009.

Kelly, Anne, *Textile Folk Art*, Batsford, 2018.

Olsson, Annhelen, *Yllebroderier: Berattande folkkonstfran Norden*, Hemslojdens forlag, 2010.

Pattullo, Mandy, *Textile Collage*, Batsford, 2016.

Wellesley-Smith, Claire, *Slow Stitch: Mindful and Contemplative Textile Art*, Batsford, 2015.

Suppliers

Alice Caroline for small quantities of Liberty print fabrics, alicecaroline.com

Cloth House for interesting fabrics including indigo, block-printed textiles and sometimes old ethnic embroideries, clothhouse.com

Colourcraft for Brusho, colourcraftltd.com

Deborah Greensill for French finds, instagram.com/dsg1964

Donna Flower Vintage for vintage fabrics and quilt pieces, www.donnaflowervintage.com

Empress Mills for silk and linen embroidery thread, empressmills.co.uk

French General for cotton fabrics including collections based on French archive designs, frenchgeneral.com

John James Needles for best British sewing needles, jjneedles.com

Linladan for vintage linen and cotton embroidery threads, linladan.com

Merchant and Mills for beautifully packaged pins and other stitching notions, merchantandmills.com

Sallie Ead for antique and rare textiles, instagram.com/sallieead

Wendy Shaw for vintage textiles and other ephemera, instagram.com/ticking_stripes

Welsh Quilt Centre for antique quilts and small pieces of quilt, welshquilts.com

Below: Suffolk puffs made from commemorative handkerchiefs.

Index

Right: *King*, 2018,
45 x 55cm
(18 x 21½in).
Mixed media.

Acknowledgements

Thank you to all the artists who kindly contributed photographs and information to support my text. You have enabled this book to be even more colourful and interesting.

Thank you also to Kristy Richardson at Batsford for supporting me all the way and to Michael Wicks for his sensitivity in photographing my work.

My husband Andrew has, as always, offered loving and full support to this project and everything else I do.

Lastly, I would like to acknowledge the role the women in my past, my mother and grandmother, have contributed to my love of sewing. I hope I am an inspiration to my daughter and grand daughter.

All images by Michael Wicks except for the following:
Edie Rose Ashley page 39, Lois Blackburn page 115,
Roger Clive-Powell page 43, Michael Graham page 112,
Phillip Jackson page 87, Hannah Lamb page 25,
Mandy Pattullo page 6, 7, 11, 14–15, 20–21, 24, 58, 69,
88 and 116–118, Luke Scott page 57, Ulla-Stina Wikander
page 66–67 and Joanne Withers page 83.

Left: 'Lace Book', 2017. Lace and fabric attached to wool blanket pages with additional embroidery.